LAODICEA

Presented To:

From:

Date:

LAODICEA

WHY THE WORLD IS NOT YET READY FOR THE SECOND COMING

Find Out and Realize
the One and Only End-Time Instruction
in Fulfillment
of What Was
Foretold

B. LISING

PARTRIDGE
A Penguin Random House Company

www.partridgepublishing.com/singapore

Contents

Introduction: How do we prepare for the Last Days? ix

Chapter 1   Only One Message 1

Chapter 2   Final Conflict... 6

Chapter 3   Four Kinds of Teaching 12

Chapter 4   Beginning and Ending of Time 32

Chapter 5   Perfect God and Perfect You 38

Chapter 6   Before the Beginning of Time...................... 43

Chapter 7   Today is the Day.. 54

Chapter 8   Bound to Disobedience................................. 60

Chapter 9   The Year of Jubilee..69

Chapter 10   Only One Prophecy 75

Chapter 11   Fall of Babylon
              and Rise of New Jerusalem 94

Chapter 12   Complete Unity in the Last Days................109

Concluding Lessons: New Covenant Representations 127

Remarks from the Author 151

Dedicated to my beloved wife

Maria Lourdes

and to my wonderful children

Eleazar

Eleakim

Eleajoy

Eleagem

They are the precious companions God has given me
in this temporary world.

*This book
is for God's
chosen people,
whose names have been written in the
Book of Life belonging to the Lamb
that was slain
from the
creation of
the world
before the
beginning
of time.*

INTRODUCTION

HOW DO WE PREPARE FOR THE LAST DAYS?

Whenever the world encounters extraordinary events like earthquakes, tsunamis, disease outbreaks, pestilence, war, falling meteors, or other phenomenal heavenly wonders, the most likely reaction is for some to say: "The end is near" or "The Second Coming is at hand." This is not surprising. What is surprising and unexpected is that God's people have the same reaction.

If we truly want to know that the Second Coming is near, all we need to do is look at the current condition of the church.

Why is the world not yet ready for the Second Coming? The reason is *Laodicea*! Too many writers, preachers, and scholars have attempted to unlock the meaning behind the word, but many, if not all, have failed to give satisfying answers. The world is not yet ready because the church is not yet prepared. The very reason the Lord Jesus will come back is for the bride—a ready church that is united, without spot, and without blemish.

The word *Laodicea* is formed from two Greek words: Laos, which means "people," and dike, which means "principle or decision."

The seventh and final letter to the churches of ancient Asia Minor is to the church in the city of Laodicea. This last message is stated as follows:

> To the angel of the church in Laodicea write: These are the words of the Amen, the faithful and true witness, the ruler of God's creation. I know your deeds, that you are neither cold nor hot. I wish you were either one or the other! So, because you are lukewarm—*neither hot nor cold*—I am about to spit you out of my mouth. (Revelation 3:14–16 NIV, emphasis added)

What does *neither hot nor cold* mean? Does the meaning of the word *Laodicea* have something to do with the given message? Is this message connected in any way to the messages given to the other churches?

By knowing and understanding the real message the Lord Jesus gave to the church at Laodicea, we will be able to unveil the one and only instruction God gave His people to fulfill what the prophecies of old foretold.

The purpose of this book is to help the church realize and understand the Lord Jesus's one and only message before His Second Coming. To do so, we must keep in mind three things:

(1) The day of the Lord is a surprise only to those in darkness but not to those who belong to the light. This can be clearly seen from the following passage:

> Now, brothers, about times and dates we do not need to write to you, for you know very well that the day of the Lord will come like a thief in the night … But you, brothers, are not in darkness so that this

day should surprise you like a thief. You are all sons of the light and sons of the day. We do not belong to the night or to the darkness. (1 Thessalonians 5:1–4 NIV)

(2) The only way we can know and understand spiritual things is through the Holy Spirit. This is strongly emphasized by the following passage:

The man without the Spirit does not accept the things that come from the Spirit of God, for they are foolishness to him, and he cannot understand them, because they are spiritually discerned. (1 Corinthians 2:14 NIV)

(3) The Lord Jesus will come back only at the time when the church is ready. This truth is revealed as follows:

Let us rejoice and be glad and give Him glory! For the wedding of the Lamb has come, and His bride has made herself ready. (Revelation 19:7 NIV)

How do we make ourselves ready for the Last Days? The best way to prepare is to do actions that are in agreement with what will happen in the Last Days. Our focus should be on events that concern the church.

Furthermore, by reading this book and through the help of the Holy Spirit, we will have a glimpse of the following:

(1) The representations of the events that took place in eternity past before the beginning of time
(2) The three major conflicts that have something to do with the two covenants

(3) The seven major stages of the journey of Israel that
    have something to do with the journey of the Lord
    Jesus and the church

By knowing and understanding these things, we will have
a comprehensible picture of the eternal gospel, which will
present to us a sensible sign about the Lord's Second Coming
that is about to happen in these Last Days.

Besides all these, this book will help us see and realize that
the Second Coming is just part of a much bigger plan that
was established by God before the beginning of time. This is
all for the sake of God's beloved chosen people, whose names
have been written in the Lamb's Book of Life.

May the Holy Spirit be our guide as we seek God's instruction
to know how to prepare for the Second Coming of our Lord
and King.

Let us now proceed.

CHAPTER 1

ONLY ONE MESSAGE

Whoever has ears, let them hear what the Spirit
says to the churches. (Revelation 2:7 NIV)

Seven specific messages were given to the seven churches
mentioned in the book of Revelation. Five churches were
given negative comments, while only two were given positive
comments. The fact that the Lord Jesus has given these negative
comments means that before His Second Coming, the church
will face a difficult stage.

But the good news is, as foretold by prophecy, the church will
eventually overcome this stage and will come to a point that
she will be ready as a bride—the point that will signal the
coming of the groom.

To be ready means to overcome, to overcome means to know
and understand first this difficult stage of the church, and
to understand this stage means to unveil the messages given
to the seven churches. If we are able to disclose the messages
behind the comments, then we will be able to know how to
prepare for the Lord's Second Coming.

The Spirit said to John the Beloved:

> Write on a scroll what you see and send it to the seven
> churches: to *Ephesus*, Smyrna, *Pergamum*, *Thyatira*,
> *Sardis*, Philadelphia and *Laodicea*. (Revelation 1:11
> NIV, emphasis added)

Notice that only two churches, Smyrna and Philadelphia,
were given positive comments; the five churches, Ephesus,
Pergamum, Thyatira, Sardis, and Laodicea, were given
negative comments. Let us look at these negative comments
and see if they are connected to each other.

- To the church in Ephesus …
  Negative comment: "I hold this against you: You
  have *forsaken your first love*." (Revelation 2:1–7 NIV,
  emphasis added)

- To the church in Pergamum …
  Negative comment: "I have a few things against you:
  You have people there who hold to the *teaching of
  Balaam*, who taught Balak to entice the Israelites to sin
  by *eating food sacrificed to idols* and by *committing sexual
  immorality*. Likewise you also have those who hold to
  the teaching of the Nicolaitans." (Revelation 2:12–17
  NIV, emphasis added)

- To the church in Thyatira …
  Negative comment: "I have this against you: You
  tolerate that woman *Jezebel*, who calls herself a
  prophetess. By *her teaching* she misleads my servants
  into *sexual immorality* and the *eating of food sacrificed
  to idols*." (Revelation 2:18–29 NIV, emphasis added)

- To the church in Sardis …
  Negative comment: "I know your deeds: You have a *reputation of being alive, but you are dead.*" (Revelation 3:1–6 NIV, emphasis added)

- To the church in Laodicea …
  Negative comment: "I know your deeds, that you are neither cold nor hot. I wish you were either one or the other! So, because you are lukewarm—*neither hot nor cold*—I am about to spit you out of my mouth." (Revelation 3:14–22 NIV, emphasis added)

To summarize, the Lord Jesus said, "I hold this against you," and, "I know your deeds":

(1) You have forsaken your first love.
(2) You hold to the teaching of Balaam.
(3) You hold to the teaching of the Nicolaitans.
(4) You hold to the teaching of Jezebel.
(5) You have a reputation of being alive, but you are dead.
(6) You are neither hot nor cold.

The teaching of Balaam is about *eating food sacrificed to idols* and *committing sexual immorality*, the teaching of the Nicolaitans is about *eating food sacrificed to idols* and *committing sexual immorality*, and the teaching of Jezebel is about *eating food sacrificed to idols* and *committing sexual immorality*. Thus the above list will become like this:

(1) Forsaken first love
(2) Eating food sacrificed to idols
(3) Committing sexual immorality
(4) Reputation of being alive but dead
(5) Neither hot nor cold

Let us now see the simple definition of each phrase:

(1) Forsaken first love: this is for married couples, one of whom forsakes the other by having an affair—having two covenants.

(2) Eating food sacrificed to idols: scripture usually refers to food as equivalent to teaching and eating as equivalent to partaking; thus, one partakes of the teaching of God and at the same time partakes of the teaching of demons—having two covenants.

(3) Committing sexual immorality: this is again for married couples, one of whom forsakes the other by having an affair—having two covenants.

(4) Reputation of being alive but being dead: scripture refers to those who eat of the fruit of the tree of life as being alive and those who eat of the fruit of the tree of the knowledge of good and evil as dead, but the phrase refers to those who eat both fruits—having two covenants.

(5) Neither hot nor cold: this simply means having two covenants.

To summarize, each item on the above list indicates having two covenants.

It should be clear by now that the five churches were given negative comments for having two covenants, and it follows that the other two churches were commended for having only one covenant. This means that the messages given to the seven churches were actually one and the same message, which makes us realize that this one message is truly very important.

What then are these two covenants? Let us read the following passage:

> Tell me, you who want to be under the law, are you not aware of what the law says? For it is written that Abraham had two sons … His son by the slave woman was born according to the flesh, but his son by the free woman was born as the result of a divine promise. These things are being taken figuratively: The women *represent two covenants* … But what does Scripture say? "*Get rid* of the slave woman and her son, for the slave woman's son *will never share* in the inheritance with the free woman's son." (Galatians 4:21–31 NIV, emphasis added)

The scripture is telling us to get rid of the former covenant, for those who belong to it will never share in the inheritance with those who belong to the latter covenant.

This is the one and only instruction the Lord Jesus has given to the church before His Second Coming. This is also the final conflict relayed in all the scripture.

We will further discuss this conflict in the next chapters and will discover how it will end in fulfillment of the prophecy.

CHAPTER 2

FINAL CONFLICT

What is obsolete and aging will soon disappear.
(Hebrews 8:13 NIV)

The former covenant is called the Old Covenant, and the latter is the New and Everlasting Covenant. These two must not and cannot be combined; there should only be one covenant, and it must be the lasting one. Scripture firmly states that the Old Covenant is already obsolete and will soon disappear. Through the blood of the Lamb, the New and Everlasting Covenant was put into effect, but the conflict arises when God's people, who were cleansed and justified by this New Covenant, still cling to the old one.

God had already declared that something was wrong with the first covenant and that He would firmly establish the New Covenant, as described in the following passage:

> For if there had been nothing wrong with that first covenant, no place would have been sought for another. But God found fault with the people and said: "The time is coming, declares the Lord, when I will make a new covenant with the house Judah … I will put my

laws in their minds and write them on their hearts.
I will be their God, and they will be my people ...
For I will forgive their wickedness and will remember
their sins no more." By calling this covenant "new,"
he has made *the first one obsolete*; and what is obsolete
and aging *will soon disappear.* (Hebrews 8:7–13 NIV,
emphasis added)

Most of the epistles written by the Apostle Paul tackle this
issue, and in the early days of the church, this problem was
already the main subject believers addressed at the meeting
recorded in Acts 15.

Paul and Barnabas were brought into sharp dispute and debate
with those who tried to mix the two covenants, as narrated in
the following passage:

Certain people came down from Judea to Antioch
and were *teaching the believers*: "Unless you are
circumcised, according to the custom taught by
Moses, you cannot be saved" ... So Paul and Barnabas
were appointed, along with some other believers, to go
up to Jerusalem to see the apostles and elders about
this question ... After much discussion, Peter got up
and addressed them: "Brothers, you know that some
time ago God made a choice among you that the
Gentiles might hear from my lips the message of the
gospel and believe ... Now then, why do you try to
test God by putting on the necks of Gentiles a yoke
that neither we nor our ancestors have been able to
bear? No! We believe it is through the grace of our
Lord Jesus that we are saved, just as they are." (Acts
15:1–11 NIV, emphasis added)

Some members of the early church believed that aside from the blood of the Lord Jesus, they still needed the blood of animals for them to be saved. The same conflict was faced by all the generations that followed—including our present generation, which we believe to be the last. We think we still need the Old Covenant, although the Lord Jesus already paid a very high price for the New Covenant. The Apostle Peter will give us the same firm answer: "No! We believe it is through the grace (and grace alone) of our Lord Jesus that we are saved"—nothing more and nothing less.

When it comes to a contract, the old one would definitely be superseded and declared void if a new one were already signed and sealed.

The Lord Jesus was born into this world to fulfill the Old Covenant, as expressed in the following passages:

> Do not think that I have come to abolish the Law or the Prophets; I have not come to abolish them *but to fulfill them*. I tell you the truth, until heaven and earth disappear, not the smallest letter, not the least stroke of a pen, will by any means disappear from the Law *until everything is accomplished*. (Matthew 5:17–18 NIV, emphasis added)

> The Law and the Prophets were proclaimed until John. Since that time, *the good news of the kingdom of God* is being preached, and everyone is forcing his way into it. (Luke 16:16 NIV, emphasis added)

> *Christ is the culmination of the law* so that there may be righteousness for everyone who believes. (Romans 10:4 NIV, emphasis added)

The word *culmination* means conclusion, finale, peak, height, zenith, result, end, and termination.

Therefore, the purpose of the Lord's First Coming is *to fulfill the Old Covenant* and to establish the New Covenant, and the purpose of the Lord's Second Coming is *to fulfill the New Covenant* and to get rid of the Old Covenant (once and for all).

The Lord will get rid of the Old Covenant once and for all because it was considered weak and useless and has made nothing perfect, as stated in the following passages:

> The *former regulation is set aside* because it was weak and useless (for the law made nothing perfect), and a better hope is introduced, by which we draw near to God. (Hebrews 7:18–19 NIV, emphasis added)

> But now, by dying to what once bound us, we have been *released from the law* so that we serve in the new way of the Spirit, and not in the old way of the written code. (Romans 7:6 NIV, emphasis added)

> But the fruit of the Spirit is love, joy, peace, patience, kindness, goodness, faithfulness, gentleness and self-control. *Against such things there is no law.* (Galatians 5:22–23 NIV, emphasis added)

> Then he said, "Here I am, I have come to do your will. *He sets aside the first to establish the second.* (Hebrews 10:9 NIV, emphasis added)

The Lord Jesus came to do the will of the Father—to set aside the Old Covenant and to establish the New and Everlasting Covenant. The main reason the Lord Jesus died on the cross was for us to be released from the Law so that we could serve in the "new way of the Spirit" (not in the old way). The conflict starts when we combine and mix the two covenants. This is the very message described in the previous chapter and as stated by the following passages:

> After beginning with the *Spirit*, are you now trying to attain your goal by *human effort*? (Galatians 3:3 NIV, emphasis added)

> No one sews a patch of unshrunk cloth on an old garment, for the patch will pull away from the garment, *making the tear worse*. Neither do people pour new wine into old wineskins. If they do, the skins *will burst*; the wine *will run out* and the wineskins *will be ruined*. No, they pour new wine into new wineskins, and both are preserved. (Matthew 9:16–17 NIV, emphasis added)

When we combine two things that must not be combined, the end result is destruction. This is the final conflict in the church, which will soon be resolved before the Second Coming of our Lord Jesus Christ. At this moment in time, the church is still inside this conflict without knowing it. The only instruction the Lord Jesus has given the church before His Second Coming is to come out of this conflict.

> *Come out of her, my people*! Run for your lives! Run from the fierce anger of the Lord. (Jeremiah 51:45 NIV, emphasis added)

> Then I heard another voice from heaven say: "*Come out of her, my people*," so that you will not share in her sins, so that you will not receive any of her plagues. (Revelation 18:4 NIV, emphasis added)

The above passages from both the Old and New Testament speak about the prophecy against Babylon. Are we now saying that Babylon is the final conflict in the church?

As foretold, New Jerusalem will soon be established; but prior to this, Babylon must first be destroyed. God's people were instructed to come out of Babylon so that they would not be destroyed along with it. Or should we say that God would not destroy Babylon if His people were still inside of it?

The following are the three major conflicts mentioned in scripture before God's people would be able to enter and fully possess the Promised Land (New Jerusalem):

(1) The Canaan conflict is the first conflict, which represents what happened before the beginning of time.
(2) The Egypt conflict is the second conflict, which represents what is happening inside of time.
(3) The Babylon conflict is the third and final conflict, which represents what will happen before the ending of time.

Israel and the church were destined to enter all these conflicts, but God had and will save His beloved people by leading them out from them.

To help us understand these conflicts, we need first to know the four kinds of teaching that exist in the world. There are supposed to be only two teachings, but the enemy devised another two, which started the conflicts. The last two teachings have caused thousands of religions and church denominations to be born into the world, and these have brought confusion to those who really seek the truth.

CHAPTER 3

FOUR KINDS OF TEACHING

Whoever eats my flesh and drinks my blood has eternal life.
(John 6:54 NIV)

Chapter 1 mentions that scripture usually refers to food as equal to teaching and eating as equal to partaking.

The saying, "You are what you eat," means that New Covenant people must eat only New Covenant teaching. In order to understand the New Covenant teaching, we need knowledge about the Old Covenant teaching as well as the other two teachings.

Let us read the following passages:

> Jesus answered, "It is written: 'Man shall not live on bread alone, but on every word that comes from the mouth of God.'" (Matthew 4:4 NIV)

> Jesus said to them, "Very truly I tell you, unless you eat the flesh of the Son of Man and drink his blood, you have no life in you. Whoever eats my flesh and drinks my blood has eternal life." (John 6:53–58 NIV)

Many of the Lord's disciples deserted Him when He gave to them these words: "Eat my flesh" and "Drink my blood." They might have been thinking: "We are not *cannibals!* But scripture is very clear: He was talking about accepting His teaching because anyone who does this is one with his teacher. And the Lord Jesus brings to us the very word that comes from the mouth of God. In fact, Jesus Himself is the Word that was from the beginning, the Word that was with God, and the Word that was God. And He is the Truth that will set us free. The word that comes from the mouth of God is the New and Everlasting Covenant teaching.

We know the Old Testament is not the Old Covenant, and the New Testament is not the New Covenant. Both the New and Old Testament contain both teachings of the two covenants. This is why we need to learn how to distinguish which is which whenever we read from this Holy Book.

The Lord Jesus's warning to the church mentioned these statements: "I hold this against you—you hold to the *teaching* of Balaam; you hold to the *teaching* of the Nicolaitans; and you hold to the *teaching* of Jezebel." This means that the church (in earlier times and at the present time) is in a condition where we actually hold to these teachings but without even noticing it.

To understand this, look at the four kinds of food (teaching) mentioned in scripture. Basically, there are only two kinds of teaching:

(1) The tree of life
(2) The tree of the knowledge of good and evil

Why then are there four? Let us see the story that took place in the Garden of Eden:

> The Lord God made all kinds of trees grow out of the ground—trees that were pleasing to the eye and good for food. In the middle of the garden were the *tree of life* and the *tree of the knowledge of good and evil*. (Genesis 2:8–9 NIV, emphasis added)

> And the Lord God commanded the man, "You are free to eat from any tree in the garden; but you must not eat from the tree of the knowledge of good and evil, for *when you eat from it you will certainly die*." (Genesis 2:15–17 NIV, emphasis added)

> Now the serpent was more crafty than any of the wild animals the Lord God had made. He said to the woman, "*Did God really say*, 'You must not eat from any tree in the garden'?" The woman said to the serpent, "We may eat fruit from the trees in the garden, but God did say, 'You must not eat fruit from the tree that is in the middle of the garden, and *you must not touch* it, or you will die.'" (Genesis 3:1–5 NIV, emphasis added)

From the above passages, we derive the four kinds of teaching:

(1) Tree of the knowledge of good and evil
(2) Tree of life
(3) Eve's "do not touch"
(4) The serpent's "did God really say"

Teaching 1: Tree of the Knowledge of Good and Evil

The "tree of the knowledge of good and evil" teaching refers to the Old Covenant (also called the teaching of Moses, the Law, the commandment, the power of sin, the law of sin and death, the ministry of condemnation and death).

The first mention of death ("you will certainly die") in the Bible is directly connected to the tree of the knowledge of good and evil; the one and only "do not do this" command of God to man is in connection with this tree ("you can eat all except this one")—failure to comply will result in sure death.

All mentions of death that follow after are directly attributed to the commandment or to the Law of Moses.

The Old Covenant has brought death, and this can be clearly seen in the following passages:

> Now if the ministry that brought death, which was engraved in letters on stone, came with glory ... will not the ministry of the Spirit be even more glorious? If the ministry that brought condemnation was glorious, how much more glorious is the ministry that brings righteousness! (2 Corinthians 3:7–11 NIV)

> Once I was alive apart from the law; but when the commandment came, sin sprang to life and I died. I found that the very commandment that was intended to bring life actually brought death ... So then, the law is holy, and the commandment is holy, righteous and good. (Romans 7:9–12 NIV)

Notice that scripture did not ever mention that this tree is evil or not good. Scripture says: "The LORD God made all kinds of trees grow out of the ground—trees that were pleasing to the eye and good for food." Everything that God created is good, and this includes the tree of the knowledge of good and evil.

The command "do not eat" specifically means "do not partake," or "have nothing to do with it," or "this is not made for you." Although this tree is considered perfect, holy, righteous, and good, it was not made for Adam and Eve. In the same way, the Old Covenant teaching is considered perfect, holy, righteous, and good. But it was never made for God's people. This is clearly stated in the following passage:

> We know that the law is good if one uses it properly. We also know that the law is made *not for the righteous* but for lawbreakers. (1 Timothy 1:8–9 NIV, emphasis added)

The fact that this tree (the Law or the commandment) is made for lawbreakers has something to do with God's judgment of sinners wherein the penalty is death. The picture of Adam and Eve having eaten from this tree portrays that all mankind (including God's people) was actually under the Old Covenant and would surely face the consequence: "you will certainly die."

The purpose of the Law is for the whole world to know sin or to be conscious of sin thus to be held accountable to God. This is plainly stated in the following passages:

> Therefore no one will be declared righteous in God's sight by the works of the law; rather, through the law we become conscious of our sin. (Romans 3:20–21 NIV)

> What shall we say, then? Is the law sinful? Certainly
> not! Nevertheless, I would not have known what sin
> was had it not been for the law. For I would not have
> known what coveting really was if the law had not said,
> "You shall not covet." But sin, seizing the opportunity
> afforded by the commandment, produced in me every
> kind of coveting. For apart from the law, sin was dead.
> (Romans 7:7–8 NIV)

Since the purpose of the Law is for us to become conscious of
sin, the ministry of condemnation is at work in our lives. We
tend to condemn ourselves and feel guilty whenever we break
a single command. Worst of it, we tend to condemn and judge
others whenever we see them committing sins. This is why
there is too much pretense and criticism not only in the world
but also within churches (those who think they are still under
the Old Covenant). The Lord Jesus said: "Do not judge before
the appointed time."

We must also emphasize that the power of sin is the Law. This
can be evidently seen in the following passages:

> The sting of *death* is sin, and the *power of sin* is the *law*.
> (1 Corinthians 15:56 NIV, emphasis added)

> What shall we conclude then? Do we have any
> advantage? Not at all! For we have already made the
> charge that Jews and Gentiles alike are *all under the
> power of sin*. (Romans 3:9–12 NIV, emphasis added)

This means that those under the Law are powerless against
sin (because sin has dominion over those who are under the
Law). They have no choice but to commit sin (because the Law

empowered them to sin) which makes the statement "you will certainly die" stand.

Scripture is very positive in stating that all have sinned:

> Therefore, just as sin entered the world through one man, and death through sin, and in this way death came to all people, because all sinned. (Romans 5:12–14 NIV)

This is the bad news: all have eaten from the tree of the knowledge of good and evil, all are under the Old Covenant, all are empowered to commit sin, all have sinned, and all therefore will die.

The good news is: "Through Christ Jesus the law of the Spirit who gives life has set you free from the law of sin and death." (Romans 8:2 NIV)

We will discuss this further in the next chapters and discover why God needed to put this tree in the Garden of Eden along with the tree of life, knowing it would bring forth the fall of man.

Teaching 2: Tree of Life

The "tree of life" teaching refers to the New Covenant (also called the gospel of life, the law of the Spirit, the ministry of the Spirit, the ministry of righteousness, the good news of the kingdom, the good news of God's grace, the teaching of the apostles).

In contrast to death, the tree of life, as the name suggests, means that this tree is the source of life eternal, while all mentions of life in the Bible are directly attributed to the New Covenant.

The New Covenant has brought life, and this can be clearly seen in the following passages:

> This grace was given us in Christ Jesus before the beginning of time, but it has now been revealed through the appearing of our Savior, Christ Jesus, who has destroyed death and has brought life and immortality to light through the gospel. (2 Timothy 1:9–10 NIV)

> Now if the ministry that brought death, which was engraved in letters on stone, came with glory ... will not the *ministry of the Spirit* be even more glorious? If the ministry that brought condemnation was glorious, how much more glorious is the *ministry that brings righteousness*! (2 Corinthians 3:7–11 NIV, emphasis added)

We are now under the ministry of righteousness. This means "there is now no condemnation for those who are in Christ Jesus." No more pretense, no more criticism, no more judging others, and no more need to feel guilty—all because we are under the ministry of the Holy Spirit and under grace.

To be more specific, the tree of life is none other than the Lord Jesus Himself because He is the source of life, and He wants us to eat from Him and have life as stated in the following passage:

> Whoever eats my flesh and drinks my blood has eternal life. (John 6:53–58 NIV)

We must notice that before scripture mentioned the tree of the knowledge of good and evil, the tree of life was mentioned first. It is the Lord's intention for man to partake of the New Covenant to have eternal life and not of the Old Covenant to end up in death.

This is the Canaan conflict, which is the first conflict, as mentioned in chapter 2. This represents that while it was God's promise to the people of Israel that this land was their inheritance, they still could not possess it because the Canaanites were still living there. In the same way, the tree of life is our real inheritance, but somehow the tree of the knowledge of good and evil came to the picture thus delaying our inheritance.

We may be asking: Does God still need to put the tree of the knowledge of good and evil or the Old Covenant in the picture if His intention is for man to have life? Why would He put something there that would cause death? We need to see the whole picture in order to see God's purpose for this, which we will see in the next chapters.

Teaching 3: Eve's "Do Not Touch"

Eve's "do not touch" teaching refers to combining Old Covenant teaching with human traditions (also called the yeast of the Pharisees and Sadducees, no-authority teaching, lowered standard of God's Law, or world religions).

Let us read the following passage:

> Since you died with Christ to the elemental spiritual forces of this world, why, as though you still belonged to the world, do you submit to its rules: "Do not handle! Do not taste! *Do not touch*!"? These rules, which have to do with things that are all destined to perish with

use, are *based on merely human commands and teachings.*
(Colossians 2:20–23 NIV, emphasis added)

Scripture states that we will be declared righteous if we obey
the Law as mentioned in this passage:

> For it is not those who hear the law who are righteous
> in God's sight, but it is those who obey the law who will
> be declared righteous. (Romans 2:13 NIV)

But the problem is that scripture also states that no one can
actually obey this Law, thus no one will be declared righteous.
In fact, this Law is with perfect standard so that there is no
way that anyone can fully obey it.

Let us read the following passages:

> For whoever keeps the whole law and yet stumbles at
> just one point is guilty of breaking all of it. (James
> 2:10–11 NIV)

> For all have sinned and fall short of the glory of God.
> (Romans 3:23 NIV)

"All have sinned" means all have failed to keep or follow
the whole Law. However, man was able to find a way and
convinced himself that he could fully obey this Law and be
declared righteous—he combined it with human traditions—
so that he would not fall short of it.

Remember the story of a certain rich ruler?

> A certain ruler asked him, "Good teacher, what
> must I do to inherit eternal life?" … You know the

commandments: "You shall not commit adultery, you shall not murder, you shall not steal, you shall not give false testimony, honor your father and mother." "All these I have kept since I was a boy," he said. When Jesus heard this, he said to him, "You still lack one thing." (Luke 18:18–27 NIV)

This man was very much sure and proud to say that he was able to keep the whole Law. Little did he know that the Law he kept was already contaminated with human commands and traditions that made its standard low so it could become possible for man to follow.

These contaminations of the Law had always been ascribed as the doings of the Pharisees and the teachers of the law. The Lord Jesus proceeded to bring back the high and perfect standard of the Law by giving these statements:

You have heard that it was said to the people long ago, "You shall not murder, and anyone who murders will be subject to judgment." But I tell you that *anyone who is angry with a brother or sister will be subject to judgment.* (Matthew 5:20–22 NIV, emphasis added)

You have heard that it was said, "You shall not commit adultery." But I tell you that *anyone who looks at a woman lustfully has already committed adultery with her in his heart.* If your right eye causes you to stumble, *gouge it out* and throw it away … And if your right hand causes you to stumble, *cut it off* and throw it away. (Matthew 5:27–30 NIV, emphasis added)

For a man just to be angry with his brother or sister already makes him a murderer. For a man just to look with lust at a woman already makes him an adulterer. To gouge out our right eye and to cut off our right hand if these cause us to stumble—these are all so hard and impossible to follow. With these set standards, everyone is sure to falter.

With regards to the Pharisees and Sadducees, the Lord Jesus gave this warning to His disciples:

> Be on your guard against the *yeast* of the Pharisees and Sadducees … Then they understood that he was not telling them to guard against the yeast used in bread, but against the *teaching* of the Pharisees and Sadducees. (Matthew 16:5–12 NIV, emphasis added)

The yeast of the Pharisees and Sadducees contaminated the Law with human traditions thus lowering the standard and rendering it without authority as stated by this passage:

> The people were amazed at his teaching, because he taught them as one who had authority, not as the teachers of the law. (Mark 1:21–22 NIV)

With this lowered standard and no-authority teaching, man began to think that he could obey the whole Law and could become righteous with his own effort. He did not then see his real need—the need for the Savior.

This is the reason why the Lord Jesus spoke so harshly against the Pharisees and the teachers of the law. Let us see the seven woes that were spoken against them:

(1) First woe: "Woe to you, teachers of the law and Pharisees, you hypocrites!"

Reason: "You shut the door of the kingdom of heaven in people's faces. You yourselves do not enter, nor will you let those enter who are trying to."

(2) Second woe: "Woe to you, teachers of the law and Pharisees, you hypocrites!"
Reason: "You travel over land and sea to win a single convert, and when you have succeeded, you make them twice as much a child of hell as you are."

(3) Third woe: "Woe to you, blind guides!"
Reason: "You say, 'If anyone swears by the temple, it means nothing; but anyone who swears by the gold of the temple is bound by that oath.' ... You also say, 'If anyone swears by the altar, it means nothing; but anyone who swears by the gift on the altar is bound by that oath.'"

(4) Fourth woe: "Woe to you, teachers of the law and Pharisees, you hypocrites!"
Reason: "You give a tenth of your spices—mint, dill and cumin. But you have neglected the more important matters of the law—justice, mercy and faithfulness."

(5) Fifth woe: "Woe to you, teachers of the law and Pharisees, you hypocrites!"
Reason: "You clean the outside of the cup and dish, but inside they are full of greed and self-indulgence."

(6) Sixth woe: "Woe to you, teachers of the law and Pharisees, you hypocrites!"
Reason: "You are like whitewashed tombs which look beautiful on the outside but on the inside are full of the bones of the dead and everything unclean. In

the same way, on the outside you appear to people as righteous but on the inside you are full of hypocrisy and wickedness."

(7) Seventh woe: "Woe to you, teachers of the law and Pharisees, you hypocrites!"
Reason: "You build tombs for the prophets and decorate the graves of the righteous ... So you testify against yourselves that you are the descendants of those who murdered the prophets."

The seven woes spoken against the Pharisees and teachers of the law prove that mixing the Old Covenant with human traditions is really a great deal to the Lord Jesus. It was a great deal when the serpent succeeded in tempting Eve to partake of the tree of the knowledge of good and evil upon hearing her add "you must not touch" to the words "you must not eat." It was a great deal that the Pharisees and teachers of the law (who were entrusted with the Law) added human commands and traditions to it.

The Pharisees and teachers of the law were actually doing the work of Satan (the serpent)—the very reason why the Lord Jesus, after pronouncing the seven woes, proceeded to say: "You snakes! You brood of vipers! How will you escape being condemned to hell?"

All peoples and religions of every nation are guilty of holding to the "do not touch" teaching. The whole world, from the very beginning of time, is actually under the Old Covenant (God's Law, with highest standard) but combined with human traditions (lowering the standard) thus giving birth to all kinds of world religions. Take note that all religions teach their members to be kind and righteous, to be better persons, to be perfect in good deeds, to avoid wrongdoing, and to abhor evil (using human effort). No religion will ever teach anyone to be sinful or to be wayward.

This may sound good, but we do not perceive the problem, because people tend to be self-righteous and miss the very purpose of the Law. Through the Law, we discover that we cannot, in any way, obey the commandments, thus we see the need for the Savior.

But if we think we can obey the Law (religion with low standard), then we will no longer see the need for the New and Everlasting Covenant to be saved.

This is the Egypt conflict, which is the second conflict, as mentioned in chapter 2. This represents that while it was God's intention for Israel to enter the land of its inheritance, it still needed to pass through the wilderness, because in the people's hearts, they were still slaves of Egypt. In the wilderness many of them died because they were not able to see the purpose of the Old Covenant (the Law). Their hearts were inclined to go back to Egypt. In the same way, we were not able to see the purpose of the tree of the knowledge of good and evil because of Eve's "do not touch" teaching (slavery to worldliness and human traditions) thus delaying us from our real inheritance—the tree of life.

Just like the Pharisees and teachers of the law, they were experts on the Law and had known from the Law that the Savior would be coming to save the nation Israel. But when the Savior came, right in front of them, of all people they were not able to recognize Him. In the same way, in the Last Days, there will be religious leaders and teachers who are zealous for God and expert on their own self-righteousness teachings but will fail to recognize the Second Coming of our Lord Jesus (and the Lord will tell them plainly: "I never knew you!").

Let us read the following passage:

> Brothers and sisters, my heart's desire and prayer to God for the Israelites is that they may be saved. For I can testify about them that they are zealous for God, but their zeal is not based on knowledge. Since *they did not know the righteousness of God and sought to establish their own*, they did not submit to God's righteousness. (Romans 10:1–4 NIV, emphasis added)

Teaching 4: The Serpent's "Did God Really Say"

The serpent's "did God really say" teaching refers to combining the New Covenant teaching with the Old Covenant teaching (also called the serpent's deception, food sacrificed to idols, or the teaching of demons). This is also the mixture or combination of all the first three teachings.

God's chosen people are the only people who can be guilty of holding to this kind of teaching. We are under the New Covenant, but the serpent has managed to deceive us to combine it with the Old Covenant or with human traditions.

This is the skillful work of Satan from the very start until the end of time—to deceive God's people who belong to the tree of life and to partake of the tree of the knowledge of good and evil and die.

This is the Babylon conflict, which is the third and final conflict in the church before the Second Coming, as discussed in chapter 2, and the very message, as discussed in chapter 1:

(1) You have forsaken your first love.
(2) You hold to the teaching of Balaam.
(3) You hold to the teaching of the Nicolaitans.
(4) You hold to the teaching of Jezebel.
(5) You have a reputation of being alive, but you are dead.
(6) You are neither hot nor cold.

Notice that after Adam and Eve ate from the forbidden tree, God immediately took a necessary step.

Let us read the following passage:

> And the Lord God said, "The man has now become like one of us, knowing good and evil. He must not be allowed to reach out his hand and take also from the tree of life and eat, and live forever" ... After he drove the man out, he placed on the east side of the Garden of Eden cherubim and *a flaming sword flashing back and forth* to guard the way to the tree of life. (Genesis 3:22–24 NIV, emphasis added)

There are so many things we know in this life that exist together but cannot mix together. In the same way, the New Covenant must not be contaminated with the Old Covenant, because life and death exist together but cannot combine or mix together. Once man partakes of the tree of the knowledge of good and evil, he will not be allowed to partake of the tree of life. A flaming sword flashing back and forth represents how hopeless and impossible the situation of man has become.

But because of the grace and love of our God, He made the supreme sacrifice so that His people could be free from the tree of the knowledge of good and evil and partake of the tree of life and live.

Our God has become not only our Creator but also our Savior. But this is no easy matter—like passing through the flaming sword that flashes back and forth. We must note that it required a very high price in order to accomplish this—the precious blood of our Lord Jesus (the Sacrificial Lamb).

Let us read the following passages:

> The next day John saw Jesus coming toward him and said, "Look, the Lamb of God, who takes away the sin of the world!" (John 1:29 NIV)

> Drink from it, all of you. This is my blood of the new covenant, which is poured out for many for the forgiveness of sins. (Matthew 26:26–28 NIV)

The Lord Jesus, knowing beforehand of how much He would suffer, was heard saying, "My God, my God, why have you forsaken me?" Afterward, His body was beaten beyond recognition, and His blood filled the streets while He carried a wooden cross—a picture of great suffering while marching toward His death. He suffered physically and experienced the torments of hell for three days and three nights—the price He needed to pay just for us to be free from the Old Covenant and be part of the New Covenant. The Old Covenant required an unusual ransom (the righteous blood of the Lamb) for us to be free from it as stated in the following passage:

> For this reason Christ is the mediator of a *new covenant*, that those who are called may receive the promised eternal inheritance—now that he has died as a ransom *to set them free from the sins committed under the first covenant*. (Hebrews 9:15 NIV, emphasis added)

Knowing this fact, the church still did not understand and was continuously being deceived by the serpent. The gospel being preached is no longer pure but contaminated—there is a mixture of the New Covenant teaching and the Old Covenant teaching. We combine faith and human effort; we mix grace and works, giving birth to all kinds of church denominations.

What the church did not know and understand until now is that this mixture or contamination of the gospel is actually a fulfillment of the prophecy. That same prophecy declared that the church would eventually come to realize this deception and soon preach the pure gospel. This will mark the end of time as revealed by this passage:

> And *this gospel of the kingdom* will be preached in the whole world as a testimony to all nations, and *then the end will come.* (Matthew 24:14 NIV, emphasis added)

We will discuss more about this prophecy in the next chapters and learn that our God is indeed almighty and in full control.

To summarize, the four kinds of teaching are as follows:

(1) The tree of the knowledge of good and evil
  • The Old Covenant teaching
  • The teaching of Moses
  • The Law (holy, righteous, and good)
  • The commandment
  • The power of sin
  • The law of sin and death
  • The ministry of condemnation and death

(2) The tree of life
- The New Covenant teaching
- The gospel of life
- The law of the Spirit
- The ministry of the Spirit
- The ministry of righteousness
- The good news of the kingdom
- The good news of God's grace
- The teaching of the apostles

(3) Eve's "do not touch"
- Combining the Law of God with human traditions
- Yeast of the Pharisees and Sadducees
- No-authority teaching
- Lowered standard of God's Law
- Result: numerous world religions

(4) The serpent's "did God really say"
- Combining New Covenant with Old Covenant teaching (or mixture of the first three teachings)
- The serpent's deception
- Food sacrificed to idols
- The teaching of demons
- Result: numerous church denominations

God created everything perfect and beautiful; there is no way for Him to commit any mistake. He is the source of life, and with Him there is no death. But why then did death appear in the picture?

We will discuss more of these topics in the next chapters and discover God's purpose behind these events.

CHAPTER 4

BEGINNING
AND ENDING OF TIME

He has also set eternity in the human heart; yet no one
can fathom what God has done from beginning to end.
(Ecclesiastes 3:11 NIV)

We need to see the whole picture to put all pieces of the puzzle
together. So the first thing is to have right knowledge and right
understanding of time. In fact, we were not allowed to fully
know and understand anything that was outside of time while
we were still inside of it.

The Lord Jesus said to Nicodemus:

> I have spoken to you of earthly things and you do not
> believe; how then will you believe if I speak of heavenly
> things? (John 4:12–13 NIV)

> The one who is from the earth belongs to the earth,
> and speaks as one from the earth. The one who comes
> from heaven is above all. He testifies to what he has
> seen and heard, but no one accepts his testimony. (John
> 4:31–32 NIV)

The word *time* suggests anything that is measurable—with beginning and with ending. This means that the physical world (the earth and everything we see, hear, taste, smell, or feel) evolves with one unit of measure—time.

Everything we know is temporary, with beginning and with ending. There is boundary; there is limit. Our knowledge and understanding is bounded with this limitation because we live and exist inside of time. There is expiration for everything that is inside of time, and we ourselves are of no exemption. Time itself is subject to expiration since everything that has beginning will eventually and definitely come to an end.

Let us read the following passages:

> So we fix our eyes not on what is seen, but on what is unseen, since what is seen is temporary, but what is unseen is eternal. (2 Corinthians 4:18 NIV)

> For we know that if the earthly tent we live in is destroyed, we have a building from God, an eternal house in heaven, not built by human hands. (2 Corinthians 5:1 NIV)

In contrast of time, there is eternity—without beginning and without ending—no boundary, no limitation, and no expiration. In eternity we speak of heavenly things or spiritual things—things we can never fully know or understand while we are inside of time.

The Lord Jesus had to enter inside of time in order to bring the eternal gospel to His people. However, He could not use heavenly language but spoke earthly things to explain this message from eternity. The scenario would be like this: just imagine if we have a time machine. Let us say we can go one hundred years back in time and give information to the people there about smart cellular phones, laptop computers, or other high technology gadgets. They will never understand a thing and may even say that we are out of this world (or out of our minds).

Furthermore, the scripture states:

> But the angel said to her, "Do not be afraid, Mary; you have found favor with God. You will conceive and give birth to a son, and you are to call him Jesus." (Luke 1:30–31 NIV)

This is how the Lord Jesus entered time—from the womb of a mother, although He did not come from the seed of a human father. He went through the process of human birth—from an infant into a baby, from a baby into a toddler, from a toddler into a child, from a child into a teen, and from a teen into an adult. These are all limitations; the Lord Jesus exemplified an ordinary life of an ordinary man during His early days. Although a mystery, it seems that He has no previous memory from eternity where He came from during the early stage of His stay inside of time. This might be true for all of us, but again, we cannot prove this while we are still inside of time. But when He was about to go outside of time, He showed His disciples a glimpse of the things of eternity.

Time and eternity are not matters of when but of where. To emphasize this truth further, we need to know that there is no way for us to understand the real meaning of the word *eternity*, since we are inside of time. We need to go inside of eternity to understand eternity, and since we are already inside of time, the only thing we can understand is time (and everything inside of it).

The Lord Jesus had to use physical things (things we are able see, hear, taste, smell, or feel) to make His point about heavenly things. Passages from the Bible serve the same purpose; through the help of the Holy Spirit, spiritual truths are revealed using earthly representations. This means, correspondingly, that the earthly light we know is just only a representation of the real light in eternity.

In the same way, all the things we know (everything that can be found inside of time) are all but representations of all the realities, which are found inside eternity. Our understanding of eternity will only be limited by the representation of things that are inside of time; thus, what we know are only shadows, not the realities themselves.

This is only true while we are still in this world—there are always limitations in everything. When the end of time has come, we will enter eternity, and we will see not the shadow but the reality.

Does this mean that this world (and everything in it) is not the reality? The answer is definitely yes, or else there would be no more need for the Truth to come and enter this world if we were already in the truth. The Lord Jesus Christ is the Truth from eternity, who was made flesh, entered time, and then went back to eternity (no longer with human flesh but with glorified body—an eternal, imperishable, immortal body).

This is the reality—those who belong to Him have this hope that the end of time will come so that they can enter eternity and be one with the Truth—no more limitations, no more boundaries, and no more expiration.

Let us read the following passages:

> Dear friends, now we are children of God, and what
> we will be has not yet been made known. But we know
> that when Christ appears, we shall be like him, for we
> shall see him as he is. (1 John 3:2 NIV)

> Listen, I tell you a mystery: We will not all sleep, but
> we will all be changed—in a flash, in the twinkling of
> an eye, at the last trumpet. For the trumpet will sound,
> the dead will be raised imperishable, and we will be
> changed. For the perishable must clothe itself with
> the imperishable, and the mortal with immortality. (1
> Corinthians 15:51–53 NIV)

We have physical eyes to see physical things, but we need
spiritual eyes to see spiritual things—no object of time will
ever enter eternity. When the end of time comes, we will
enter eternity. But we will be given an eternal, imperishable,
immortal body just like our Savior and Lord Jesus Christ so
that we shall see Him as He is.

For the meantime (while waiting for the ending of time), let us
first discover the reason why there is beginning of time.

Why does time need to exist if there is already eternity in the
first place? The answer to this question will enable us to see
the whole picture and will give us a clear understanding of the
eternal gospel. The gospel came from eternity—it is before the
beginning of time and encompasses even after the ending of
time, as described in the following passage:

> Then I saw another angel flying in midair, and he had
> the *eternal gospel* to proclaim to those who live on the

earth—to every nation, tribe, language and people. (Revelation 14:6 NIV, emphasis added)

In eternity there is no such word as *eternity past* or *eternity future*—only *eternity*. But in order to have a representation in knowing and understanding how the gospel came from eternity, we have to use our understanding of time and equate it with eternity (shadow–reality representation). We need also to stress that the real time is actually the eternity (which we cannot understand) and the time (which we know and understand) is actually not the reality. So for the sake of representation, let us use the following definitions:

> Eternity past = before the beginning of time
> Eternity future = after the ending of time

We will discuss this further in the following chapters, but let us first read a short story in the next chapter that gives us an overview about the gospel.

This story is for God's chosen people, whose names have been written in the Book of Life belonging to the Lamb that was slain from the creation of the world before the beginning of time. This is for you.

Chapter 5

Perfect God and Perfect You

Dear friends, now we are children of God, and
what we will be has not yet been made known.
(1 John 3:2 NIV)

This is the story from eternity past before the creation of man:

> God is perfect—everything He does is perfect. He is
> full of beauty, of joy, and of holiness. God is good—
> everything He does is good. God is love—He does
> everything in love. And perfect love needs to be shared.
> God is one—there is the Father, there is Jesus, there is
> the Spirit—in perfect unity.

> God is God—He needs to create, He needs to share
> His love, He needs to show His goodness, He needs to
> express His joy. God needs people who will be called
> God's people—created in His own image, after His
> own likeness—who will be one with Him, who will
> reciprocate His love, who will revere and worship Him,
> who will reign with Him, who will be an extension of
> His love and of His goodness and of His joy.

God is the beginning and the end. He is eternally sovereign, almighty, all-powerful, omnipresent, all knowing, and with perfect wisdom. He knows the past, He knows the present, He knows the future, and He does everything in perfect order.

And God considered the perfect plan of creation.

Initially, He set up His throne in heaven and created numerous perfect angels who would love and serve Him and who would love and serve His people as well.

God saw all that He had made, and it was all very good. But when He looked deeply into the future, He was saddened. He saw His most perfect angel would rebel against Him, He saw one-third of His numerous beautiful angels would follow in rebellion, and He saw Hades and hell would be formed because of them.

Then God asked: "Shall we proceed in creating man?" But when God looked more deeply into the future, He was filled with joy and said: "Yes! Let us proceed in creating man."

Why? Because behold He saw the perfect you.

Secondly, He set up the earth as His footstool and created in perfect order the light, sky, land and seas, plants and trees, sun and moon and stars, fish and birds, livestock and wild animals, and finally man and woman.

God saw all that He had made, and it was all very good. But when He looked deeply into the future, He felt very sad. He saw man would choose his own way instead of God's way; He saw earthquakes, famines, pestilences, wars, and chaos; and He saw man would suffer sicknesses, afflictions, problems, grief, pain, and even death.

Then God asked: "Shall we proceed in creating man?" But when God looked more deeply into the future, He was filled with joy and said: "Yes! Let us proceed in creating man."

Why? Because behold He saw the perfect you.

And then at that deciding moment, God asked: "What is the perfect solution for all these?"

God looked deeply into the future, and subsequently He saw the perfect solution. Then He felt so very sad and was filled with grief. The Father saw His only begotten Son carrying a wooden cross and heavily wounded. His blood filled the streets as He marched toward His death. He saw Jesus suffering the torments of hell for three days and three nights. He heard Jesus saying: "My God, my God, why have You forsaken Me?" (This is so because the sin of all mankind was laid upon Jesus's body, and the Father, in His holiness, could not look upon Him—first time in eternity that the perfect union was broken).

Then God cried out: "Shall we proceed in creating man?"

There was great silence. Then God looked extremely deep into the eternity future.

He saw and heard the voice of many angels numbering thousands upon thousands and ten thousand times ten thousand. They encircled the throne and the living creatures and the elders. In a load voice, they sang: "Worthy is the Lamb, who was slain, to receive power and wealth and wisdom and strength and honor and glory and praise!"

He saw and heard every creature—in heaven and on earth and under the earth and on the sea, and all that is in them—singing: "To Him, who sits on the throne, and to the Lamb be praise and honor and glory and power, forever and ever!"

Finally, behold, He saw the perfect you—without spot and without blemish—perfectly united with the Father, with the Son, and with the Holy Spirit, sharing His goodness, His love, and His joy and seated with Him on His throne, reigning with Him forevermore.

When God saw all these, He was filled with joy and exclaimed: "Yes! Let us now surely proceed in creating man."

Why? Because behold the perfect God saw the perfect you.

And so is the beginning of creation. Amen!

God is perfect. This means He cannot make a mistake, particularly on the choices He has made or will make. He did not make a mistake when He chose to create Lucifer, although He already knew that he would rebel against Him—as well as one-third of the population of angels who followed in rebellion.

All that was created constituted the perfect creation—the heavens, the earth, the angels, the exact numbers—these were all included. God cannot create more or less—always exact—because God is perfect.

This is the one truth that was firmly established in eternity—the perfect God did not make a mistake in creating you!

CHAPTER 6

BEFORE THE BEGINNING OF TIME

We declare God's wisdom, a mystery that has been hidden
and that God destined for our glory before time began.
(1 Corinthians 2:7 NIV)

Why does time need to exist if there is already eternity in the
first place? What happened in eternity past so much so that
time needed to begin?

For sure, God created time—for what purpose?

As mentioned previously, the answers to these questions will
enable us to see the whole picture and will give us a clear
understanding of the eternal gospel.

Again, we need to understand that God, our Creator, lives and
operates inside of eternity while we live and operate inside of
time, and there is a very big difference in the system of how
we think, see, feel, or move.

To see this point, let us read the following passages:

> But do not forget this one thing, dear friends: With the Lord *a day is like a thousand years*, and *a thousand years are like a day.* (2 Peter 3:8 NIV, emphasis added)

> What has been will be again, what has been done will be done again; *there is nothing new under the sun.* (Ecclesiastes 1:9–10 NIV, emphasis added)

> *There is a time for everything,* and a season for every activity under the heavens: a time to be born and a time to die. (Ecclesiastes 3:1–8 NIV, emphasis added)

> From one man he made all the nations, that they should inhabit the whole earth; and he *marked out their appointed times* in history and the boundaries of their lands. (Acts 17:26 NIV, emphasis added)

> To this John replied, "A person *can receive only what is given them from heaven.*" (John 3:27 NIV, emphasis added)

> The *eyes of the LORD are on the righteous,* and his ears are attentive to their cry. (Psalms 34:15 NIV, emphasis added)

> For he chose us in him *before the creation of the world* to be holy. (Ephesians 1:4 NIV, emphasis added)

> *Before I formed you* in the womb I knew you, *before you were born* I set you apart. (Jeremiah 1:5 NIV, emphasis added)

This grace was given us in Christ Jesus *before the beginning of time.* (2 Timothy 1:9–10 NIV, emphasis added)

In the hope of eternal life, which God, who does not lie, promised *before the beginning of time.* (Titus 1:1–3 NIV, emphasis added)

The inhabitants of the earth *whose names have not been written in the book of life from the creation of the world* will be astonished when they see the beast. (Revelation 17:8 NIV, emphasis added)

All inhabitants of the earth will worship the beast—all whose names have not been written in the Lamb's book of life, *the Lamb who was slain from the creation of the world.* (Revelation 13:8 NIV, emphasis added)

From eternity, God is in full control of what has happened and what will happen inside of time. Notice the emphasized phrases from the above passages. We can easily conclude that before anything will happen inside of time, something already took place before the beginning of time (or before the creation of the world, which we will call the eternity past).

Every event or thing that has happened or will happen inside of time was actually determined or is being determined by whatever happened or decided inside the eternity past.

Let us emphasize the following from the above passages:

(1) The Lamb was already slain even before the world was created (the ultimate sacrifice was already made even before time existed).

(2) The writing or not writing (inclusion or exclusion) of names in the Lamb's Book of Life was already decided and finalized before time existed.

(3) Eternal life is a gift from God, but the promise of that life was made before the beginning of time.

(4) Grace was already given us in Christ Jesus before the beginning of time.

(5) Before we were formed in the womb, the Lord already knew us; we were already set apart before birth.

(6) We were already chosen in Him, before the creation of the world, to be holy and blameless in His sight.

(7) God decided what country we would be born in and on what date. (It was never by chance, and it is always according to God's purpose.)

(8) We can receive only what is given us from heaven.

(9) There is an appointed time for everything and a season for every activity under the heavens.

(10) There is nothing new under the sun. (Everything is a repeated process while inside of time.)

(11) The eyes of the Lord are always upon us, and His ears are always attentive to our prayers.

(12) God indeed is almighty and in full control.

The gospel is actually a message portraying the good thing that happened inside the eternity past. This is why the gospel is called the eternal gospel. It came from eternity.

From eternity, something not good happened. But because of God's love and mercy, He caused something good to happen—this is the gospel (the good news). But since we cannot fully understand the things of eternity while inside of time, the message of the gospel will only be understood as a shadow of the reality; that is, the events that happened in the eternity past were being explained by the earthly representations offered by scripture. This means that all characters, stories, or events that were mentioned in the Bible are all shadows of the reality.

The good thing is that with the help of the Holy Spirit and as we continue to read and study the Bible, we will soon discover that there is simply and actually only one message, one prophecy, one instruction, one interpretation, and one journey to take—because God is one.

Let us read the following passage:

> Hear, O Israel: The LORD our God, the LORD is one. (Deuteronomy 6:4 NIV)

God is one. For now this may not mean a lot to you, but this statement says it all. We need to understand this truth so that we can have a grasp of the gospel that took place in eternity past. God is one. It all started with this truth, and it will all end with this truth.

In eternity past and from the very beginning, all is one with God because God is one. All was made by God, and all was created perfect and beautiful. God is light, and all that is one with Him is in the light and has light. God is life, and all that is one with Him has life. God is good, and all that is one with Him shares His goodness. Love binds all together because God is love, and there is joy everywhere because all is one with the Creator.

Consequently, all that is not one with God will become the opposite because God is one. God is light, and all that is not one with Him will be in darkness. God is life, and all that is not one with Him will die. God is good, and all that is not one with Him will become evil. God did not create evil, death, or darkness. Darkness is the absence of God because God is light. Death is the absence of God because God is life. Evil is the absence of God because God is good and holy.

Let us read the following passage:

> I am the vine; you are the branches. If you remain in me and I in you, you will bear much fruit; *apart from me you can do nothing.* (John 15:5 NIV, emphasis added)

We were created to be one with God because God is one. God has chosen us to be one with Him because He wants us to have life, not death; to be in the light, not in darkness; and to be holy, not evil. He does not want us to be separated from Him, because He loves us eternally and because God is love.

As long as all is one with God, there will be no problem. But as we all know it, this has not been the case. God had known from the very beginning that as soon as He considered the creation of man, everything would be thrown into chaos.

Our Creator was never surprised with the rebellion of angels, especially of the archangel Lucifer turned Satan. As narrated in chapter 5 of this book, God chose to proceed in creating man, although He knew very well that it would require a very high price to set all things right after the creation.

Our God indeed deserves all glory and honor and praise and adoration and worship because He chose to create us in spite of all these things. The plan of saving man after the creation was the major focus of our Creator, although this was very costly on His part (but He did it anyway). All our thanks and eternal gratitude belongs to Him because He is now not only our Creator but also our Savior as well.

Let us now take a look at a shadow story to give us a glimpse of the things that took place in eternity past:

> God is the beginning and the end. It all started with Him, and it will all end with Him. He lives in eternity and has created all the heavens along with all the holy angels in preparation for His biggest plan of all—the creation of mankind (to be created in His own image, after His own likeness—His treasured people, the apples of His eyes, the heirs of His kingdom, and His corulers of all His vast creations).

> There is only one rule to follow—to be one with the Creator—because God is one.

> This rule is for the good of all His living creations because no one can truly live if separated from the Source of life. This is the covenant of life that will be followed for all eternity. But God knew from the start that the angel Lucifer and one-third of the angels would break this rule. Lucifer, who became Satan (the serpent or the devil), will eventually devise a plan that will surely deceive God's beloved people to reject the Eternal Covenant and choose another covenant that will cause them to be separated from the Source of life.

> Knowing this fact, God had beforehand made the perfect plan of salvation but at the expense of His most beloved, only begotten Son. This He had done because of His great love for His people (God the Father and God the Son along with the Holy Spirit had done this full heartedly and with great wisdom).

When that moment in eternity came for God's people to break the Eternal Covenant and before they could be separated eternally from the Creator, the perfect plan of salvation was put into effect. The Lamb was slain, and eternity was put into a temporary halt, causing the ticking of time to begin.

God knew that not all of His precious people would accept this act of grace, so He took a book and wrote down all the names of those who would and will be saved. God called this book the Lamb's Book of Life. The names of those who have rejected Him both as Creator and as Savior were not written on this book, and they will all be judged and separated from Him eternally, just like the devil and all the angels who rebelled against Him.

Thus the time began. The world was created, and the whole of mankind was placed as a seed in the first man, Adam. The history of man started, and each would be born (and die) at his own appointed time and place according to God's plan and purpose. A person can receive only what is given from heaven. God has appointed time for everything and a season for every activity under the heavens. There is nothing new under the sun—everything is a repeated process while inside of time.

But the eyes of the Lord are upon all His righteous people. Although they will experience all sorts of hardship and suffering, the Lord is watching over them with favor day and night.

God caused the first part of man's history to be recorded in a book (called scripture). All characters, stories, or

events that were mentioned relay the same message—
the love of God the Father through the sacrifice of His
only begotten Son and the work of the Holy Spirit—
instructing God's people to come back to the Creator
by choosing the Eternal Covenant.

God's chosen people, whose names have been written
in the Lamb's Book of Life, will come to understand
and believe this message. Then again, those whose
names were not written in the Lamb's Book of Life will
never understand and believe this message. They have
rejected the Eternal Covenant, they have rejected God
as their Creator, and they have rejected God as their
Savior—so God will reject them.

Those who have understood and believed the message
(while inside of time) will first become one with
the Holy Spirit. This is the first stage of the plan of
salvation.

When the number of the chosen people, whose names
have been written in Lamb's Book of Life, has been
completed, the wedding of the Lamb will take place. This
is where the chosen people (the church), who are one with
the Holy Spirit, will become one with God the Son (the
Lord Jesus)—the second stage of the plan of salvation.

This will signal the ending of time and will cause the
eternity future to begin—the third and final stage of
the plan of salvation, where those who are one with the
Holy Spirit and the Lord Jesus will become one with
God the Father. Thus the Eternal Covenant will be
fulfilled, and all will become one with God because
God is one.

God waits patiently for all His beloved chosen heirs to be one with Him once again and forevermore, never to be separated from Him. They will worship Him and reign with Him in eternity. Together as one with God, a very exciting life awaits His people—the one true life everlasting, which cannot be described and no human mind has been able to conceive—beyond comprehension while still inside of time. This is the Eternal Gospel—the perfect plan of salvation. Amen!

This is only a shadow story. The events mentioned in this story are only shadows of what really happened in eternity past. There is no way for us (as people of time) to fully know and understand those events. We really do not know the things of eternity that were involved in the story—the thing that caused us to be separated from our Creator or the thing that will cause us to be one again with Him. But the Holy Spirit (our Teacher) uses scripture to reveal and give us a glimpse of the truth.

Let us read the following passages:

> We do, however, speak *a message of wisdom among the mature*, but not the wisdom of this age or of the rulers of this age, who are coming to nothing. No, we declare God's wisdom, *a mystery that has been hidden* and that God destined for our glory *before time began* ... as it is written: "*What no eye has seen, what no ear has heard, and what no human mind has conceived*"—the *things God has prepared* for those who love him. (1 Corinthians 2:4–10 NIV, emphasis added)

> Now to him who is able to establish you in accordance with my gospel, the message I proclaim about Jesus Christ, in keeping with the *revelation of the mystery*

hidden for long ages past, but now revealed and made known through the prophetic writings by the command of the eternal God, so that all the Gentiles might come to the obedience that comes from faith—to the only wise God be glory forever through Jesus Christ! Amen. (Romans 16:25–27 NIV, emphasis added)

CHAPTER 7

TODAY IS THE DAY

On the seventh day God rested from all his works.
(Hebrews 4:4 NIV)

One of the greatest stories that characteristically represents the eternal gospel is the story of the two criminals who were crucified along with the Lord Jesus, who made a most powerful statement: "Today you will be with me in paradise."

Let us read the following passages:

> *Two rebels* were crucified with him, one on his right and one on his left. Those who passed by hurled insults at him … In the same way the chief priests, the *teachers of the law* and the elders mocked him. (Matthew 27:38– 41 NIV, emphasis added)

> One of the criminals who hung there hurled insults at him: "Aren't you the Messiah? Save yourself and us!" But the other criminal rebuked him. "Don't you fear God," he said, "since you are under the same sentence? We are punished justly, for we are getting what our deeds deserve. But this man has done nothing wrong."

> Then he said, "Jesus, remember me when you come into your kingdom." Jesus answered him, "*Truly I tell you, today you will be with me in paradise.*" (Luke 23:39–43 NIV, emphasis added)

Three persons were crucified that day, and they had one thing in common—they were crucified because they were all under the Law. The cause of their death was because of the Old Covenant, which is the ministry of death and condemnation.

The teachers of the law were also there. Jesus called them snakes and a brood of vipers. They represent the serpent, whose sole purpose is to deceive mankind to eat from the tree of the knowledge of good and evil (to have them get inside the Old Covenant and remain in it). The Law is their weapon of death.

The first person who was crucified voluntarily had himself be under the Law and gladly took the penalty required by the Law to save those who are under the Law. This is our Lord and Savior Jesus Christ.

The second person was under the Law and remained under it. He did not believe in the Lord Jesus and had rejected God's act of grace. He represents those whose names have not been written in the Lamb's Book of Life, because they have rejected God as their Creator and Savior. So God rejected them, and they will be judged of eternal death.

The third and last person was under the Law but did not remain under it. He believed in the Lord Jesus and had acknowledged God not only as his Creator but also as his Savior. He is now under the New and Everlasting Covenant and represents the church—those whose names have been written in the Lamb's Book of Life. So God granted them eternal life; they will be with Him and will reign with Him forevermore. To them the Lord gave this grand promise: "Today you will be with me in paradise."

What did the Lord Jesus mean when He mentioned the word *today?*

Let us read the following passage:

> Be very careful, then, how you live—not as unwise but as wise, making the most of every opportunity, because *the days are evil.* (Ephesians 5:8–16 NIV, emphasis added)

Scripture declares that the days are evil inside of time. Not a single day was considered holy because everyone inside of time was under the Old Covenant, thus under condemnation. Everyone was darkness, evil, unholy, or unrighteous; all were under God's wrath and would soon face the judgment of eternal death. But God made a promise of hope. He would send His one and only begotten Son to be the Savior of the world.

To fulfill this promise, God has chosen and set apart one day that is to be holy (for all the days are evil). He called this day today.

Let us read the following passages:

> *God again set a certain day,* calling it "*Today.*" This he did when a long time later he spoke through David, as in the passage already quoted: "*Today,* if you hear his voice, do not harden your hearts." For if Joshua had given them rest, God would not have spoken later

> about another day. There remains, then, a *Sabbath-rest* for the people of God; for anyone who enters God's rest also rests from their works, just as God did from his. (Hebrews 4:6–11 NIV, emphasis added)

> For God says, "At just the right time, I heard you. On the day of salvation, I helped you." Indeed, the "right time" is now. *Today is the day of salvation.* (2 Corinthians 6:1–2 NLT, emphasis added)

Today is God's chosen day that will link the eternity past and the eternity future. This is the only day inside of time set apart for God's chosen people.

In this day the New Covenant people must reside and walk. In this day there is life, there is love, there is light, there is righteousness, there is joy, and there is peace. And this is where God meets His dearly loved people. This is the only day that is connected to eternity, and this is where God's people are filled with the Holy Spirit. The blessings of the Lord are ever present in this day.

While being crucified, the Lord Jesus proclaimed this day special. He proclaimed it to one of the criminals: "Truly I tell you today you will be with me in paradise." That criminal represents the church—those who were formerly under the Old Covenant but are now under the New and Everlasting Covenant and whose names have been written in the Lamb's Book of Life. They were released from the Law so that they could serve in the new way of the Spirit—all because of the grace and sacrificial love of the Lord Jesus.

This is the very fulfillment of the promise of God, as described by the following passages:

> The people walking in darkness have seen a great light;
> on those living in the *land of deep darkness* a light has
> dawned. (Isaiah 9:2 NIV, emphasis added)

> The people living in darkness have seen a great light;
> on those living in the *land of the shadow of death* a light
> has dawned. (Matthew 4:12–17 NIV, emphasis added)

Notice that scripture describes the world as the land of deep darkness or the land of the shadow of death. And the Lord Jesus came to the world (inside of time) to be the great Light for the people who were living in darkness and to be the true Life for those living in the land of the shadow of death.

As discussed in the previous chapter, all who are not one with God will become the opposite, because God is one. God is light, and all who are not one with Him will be in darkness. God is life, and all who are not one with Him will be in death. God is good, and all who are not one with Him will become evil. This is what we were before the Lord Jesus came into the world.

Knowing that fact, God made a way for man to become one with Him once more and forevermore, as mentioned by this passage:

> The virgin will conceive and give birth to a son, and
> they will call him *Immanuel* (which means "*God with
> us*"). (Matthew 1:21–23 NIV, emphasis added)

"God with us" is the greatest news ever proclaimed to mankind. This is the gospel (the good news). It means that today we have God with us. We are now light, not darkness; we now have life, not death; we are now righteous, not evil. Immanuel is most worthy of praise.

Today is also proclaimed by scripture as "a Sabbath-rest for the people of God; for anyone who enters God's rest also rests from their works, just as God did from His." The Old Covenant is about works, while the New Covenant is about rest. The former is about gaining God's favor and blessings by human effort (observing the Law), while the latter is about gaining God's favor and blessings by entering that rest (that is, by believing in the Lord Jesus who is the Lord of the Sabbath).

Today is the day of salvation and of God's favor because this is the only day (inside of time) that is under the New Covenant; all the other days are considered evil because they are all under the Old Covenant. Those who did not remain in the Old Covenant and now belong to the New Covenant have entered today. They entered God's rest, so they rested from their own works just as God did from His.

The New Covenant is also an Everlasting Covenant—which means that today is also everlasting (the only day that is a part of eternity). This is where Immanuel is (God with us). God's people were supposed to remain inside of today until the end of time. But as the prophecy foretold, the church has come out of today by combining the New Covenant teaching with the Old Covenant teaching. This is the Babylon stage, which is the final conflict in the church.

The only instruction the Lord Jesus has given the church before His Second Coming is to come out of Babylon. These we will discuss further in the concluding chapters.

CHAPTER 8

BOUND TO DISOBEDIENCE

These things happened so that the
scripture would be fulfilled.
(John 19:36 NIV)

The story of Adam and Eve in the Garden of Eden portrays the wonderful prophecy regarding the Lord Jesus and the church. It speaks of the sacrificial love the Lord has for His people, but many teachers narrate the story by pointing to Eve as the one to blame for why mankind is suffering from sin and death.

Let us read the following passage:

> When the woman saw that the fruit of the tree was good for food and pleasing to the eye, and also desirable for gaining wisdom, *she took some and ate it.* She also gave some to her husband, who was with her, and *he ate it.* (Genesis 3:6 NIV, emphasis added)

They say: "If only Eve had not desired to eat that fruit, mankind would probably have a completely different story now."

They further say: "If only Adam had not conceded to his wife, the catastrophe could have been prevented."

Others even blame God by saying: "If God had not created that tree or put the serpent there, Adam and Eve would not have been deceived or fallen from the temptation."

These assumptions are totally absurd and take the listeners away further from the truth.

In contrast, this story is actually a representation of the gospel from eternity and a prophecy that will guide God's chosen people during their stay inside of time.

Let us read the following passages:

> The man said, "This is now bone of my bones and flesh of my flesh; she shall be called 'woman,' for *she was taken out of man*." That is why a man leaves his father and mother and is united to his wife, and *they become one flesh*. (Genesis 2:23–24 NIV, emphasis added)

> For this reason a man will leave his father and mother and be united to his wife, and the two will become one flesh. *This is a profound mystery*—but I am talking about *Christ* and the *church*. (Ephesians 5:31 NIV, emphasis added)

> Nevertheless, death reigned from the time of Adam to the time of Moses, even over those who did not sin by breaking a command, as did *Adam, who is a pattern of the one to come*. (Romans 5:13–14 NIV, emphasis added)

> But when the set time had fully come, God sent his
> Son, born of a woman, *born under the law, to redeem*
> *those under the law,* that we might receive adoption to
> sonship. (Galatians 4:4–5 NIV, emphasis added)

From the above passages, scripture clearly states that the man
Adam represents the Lord Jesus, while the wife, Eve, represents
the church (God's chosen people). The prophecy states that the
two shall become one. Moreover, scripture states that Adam is
a pattern of the One to come.

From the story, Eve ate the fruit of the tree of the knowledge of
good and evil. This represents that God's chosen people have
come under the Old Covenant, subjecting them to the penalty
of death (separation from the Source of life).

Adam, because of his love for his wife, also ate the fruit
(scripture states that Eve is the one who was deceived, not
Adam). This represents the Lord Jesus coming to this world,
born under the Law to redeem those under the Law, as
mentioned in scripture. The Lord Jesus (as the Sacrificial
Lamb) gladly took the penalty of death in order for us to be
free from the Law and for us to become one once more with
the Source of life.

We will discuss this prophecy further in the next chapter, but
let us first see the reason why man is prone to disobey and to
commit sin.

From the previous chapter, we learned that everything that
has happened and will happen inside this world is actually
directly connected to whatever has happened or will happen
inside of eternity. We also learned that the gospel from eternity
is continuously being revealed from the events that have taken

place and will take place inside of time, and this we can know through the help of the Holy Spirit.

Let us read the following passages:

> For *God has bound everyone over to disobedience* so that he may have mercy on them all. (Romans 11:32 NIV, emphasis added)

> But *Scripture has locked up everything under the control of sin*, so that what was promised, being given through faith in Jesus Christ, might be given to those who believe. (Galatians 3:22 NIV, emphasis added)

> For God did not send his Son into the world to condemn the world, but to save the world through him. Whoever believes in him is not condemned, but *whoever does not believe stands condemned already* because they have not believed in the name of God's one and only Son. (John 3:17–18 NIV, emphasis added)

The above passages clearly state that God Himself bound all mankind over to disobedience and under the control of sin, which means that man had actually no choice but to disobey and commit sin.

This is a very strong statement, as if God is playing around with people. But after seeing the whole picture from the previous chapters, we were able to know and understand that God is actually relaying a message of hope to His people.

In order to do this, He needs first to make His beloved people understand their real situation—that from eternity past they were already under deep trouble that cannot be exactly explained in this world. Also, the above passage from the book of John states that man, without doing anything, stands condemned already, and the only way to get out of trouble is to believe in the name of God's one and only Son.

God has used the Law (or the Old Covenant) as a vivid representation of that deep trouble and has used grace (or the New and Everlasting Covenant) as a representation of the only solution to get out of that trouble. Along with these, the cost involved (the blood of the Lamb—the sacrifice of the Lord Jesus) to establish that perfect solution is always an integral part of those representations. All other things of this world that were used by scripture to relay the message of the eternal gospel always point to the two covenants.

The real situation that we were in before the beginning of time is compared to a debt that is impossible to pay—there is no way for us to save ourselves. God, our Creator, is the only one who can save us but not without a price—a very high price that requires the death of His only begotten Son.

Let us read the following passage:

> "Who then can be saved?" Jesus replied, "What is impossible with man is possible with God." (Luke 18:26–27 NIV)

Going back to the story of Adam and Eve in the Garden of Eden, notice the following representations:

(1) The two trees were there to represent the two covenants.
(2) The serpent was there to represent Satan (the deceiver).
(3) Eve was there to represent the church.
(4) Adam was there to represent the Lord Jesus.

(5) Adam and Eve to become one was mentioned to represent the prophecy about the wedding of the Lamb and His bride (unity between the Lord Jesus and the church).

(6) Everything was so well arranged by God to relay the message of the eternal gospel.

To emphasize, there are no reasons for us to blame Adam and Eve for their disobedience, because God had exactly arranged everything to happen this way to tell us the real situation that we were in—that from eternity past, we were already deceived by Satan and chose to break the Eternal Covenant separating us from the Source of life. We were already under judgment and were condemned to die, but God sent His only Son to save us from death. We will again become one with our Creator and Savior as promised by Him before the beginning of time.

As for those who have not acknowledged Him as their Creator and have rejected Him as their Savior, scripture has a lot to say about them:

> For since the message spoken through angels was binding, and every violation and disobedience received its just punishment, *how shall we escape if we ignore so great a salvation?* (Hebrews 2:2–3 NIV, emphasis added)

> Therefore *God gave them over* in the sinful desires of their hearts to sexual impurity for the degrading of their bodies with one another ... *God gave them over* to shameful lusts ... *God gave them over* to a depraved mind, so that they do what ought not to be done. (Romans 1:24–32 NIV, emphasis added)

All of mankind from eternity past has rejected the Eternal Covenant and has rebelled against God as Creator. This is the first rebellion. God is willing to forgive man of this ignorance, so He gave man a second chance (which is also the last chance because the required payment was the precious life of His most beloved Son—a once and for all sacrifice). It is indeed a great salvation, and as stated from the above passage, those who ignore this will never escape. This is the second rebellion.

To emphasize, the first rebellion is the rebellion against the Creator, while the second rebellion (which is also the final rebellion) is the rebellion against the Savior.

For those who have rebelled against God as their Savior, it is God Himself who gave them over to continuous disobedience and to committing unrighteous acts—things that ought not to be done. These are the people who have remained in the Old Covenant (the Law) and have rejected the New and Everlasting Covenant (God's grace). The Law is the power of sin; therefore, those who remain under the Law will always be bound to disobedience. They may not want to disobey, but still they are sanctioned to commit sin because sin has dominion over them (and this is what it means to be under the Old Covenant).

As for God's chosen people, they were once under this Law and were also bound to disobedience, but upon hearing about the Truth (the Lord Jesus) they realized that there was no way for them to be saved by observing the Law. Let us again read the following passage:

> Therefore *no one will be declared righteous* in God's sight *by the works of the law*; rather, through the law we become conscious of our sin. (Romans 3:20–21 NIV, emphasis added)

To again give emphasis, being under the Old Covenant means that we are powerless against sin. We have no choice but to commit sin (because it is the Law that empowers us to sin, and sin has dominion over us), thus death became inevitable. Seeing this situation as a shadow, the reality from eternity past would mean the following:

(1) Being separated from the Source of life would put us in eternal death.
(2) Being separated from the Source of light would put us in eternal darkness.
(3) Being separated from the Source of holiness would make us evil and cause us to do evil continuously.

The good news is it would not end for us this way because God has now positioned Himself not only as our Creator but also as our Savior. And the prophecy will surely be fulfilled—we will again become one with God because God is one. Our Creator and Savior is indeed great and awesome.

As mentioned earlier, the first purpose of God is to make us realize our real situation. By realizing our real situation, we now see our real need—the need for the Savior. This will make us stop putting up our own effort and put our trust and faith in the Truth—and the Truth shall set us free. Free from what? We were freed from the Law (the power of sin). The Lord Jesus has broken the curse and has provided the access for us to be one with the Holy Spirit while inside of time. And being one with the Holy Spirit means the following:

(1) Being one with the Source of life has granted us life instead of death.
(2) Being one with the Source of light has granted us to live and walk in the light instead of darkness.

(3) Being one with the Source of holiness has granted us freedom from the curse (sin has no more dominion over us; we are no longer bound to disobedience)— because we are no longer under the Law. We are now under the power of righteousness, so we will be doing righteous deeds.

Let us read the following passages:

> For we know, brothers loved by God, that he has chosen you, because our gospel came to you not simply with words, but also with power, with the Holy Spirit and with deep conviction. (1 Thessalonians 1:4–5 NIV)

> But we ought always to thank God for you, brothers loved by the Lord, because from the beginning God chose you to be saved through the sanctifying work of the Spirit and through belief in the truth. He called you to this through our gospel, that you might share in the glory of our Lord Jesus Christ. (2 Thessalonians 2:13–14 NIV)

CHAPTER 9

THE YEAR OF JUBILEE

Let no debt remain outstanding.
(Romans 13:8 NIV)

As mentioned from the previous chapter, the real situation that we were in before the beginning of time is compared to a debt that is impossible to pay. Therefore, it was God who made a way to cancel our debts—He sent His one and only begotten Son to die on the cross and pay the penalty for our sins. Because of this we were completely forgiven, and all our debts were paid in every respect.

Let us read the following passage:

> At the end of every seven years you must cancel debts. This is how it is to be done: Every creditor shall cancel any loan they have made to a fellow Israelite. They shall not require payment from anyone among their own people, because *the LORD's time for canceling debts has been proclaimed*. (Deuteronomy 15:1–2 NIV, emphasis added)

When the Lord Jesus died on the cross, the LORD's time for canceling debts had been proclaimed—no more debt remained outstanding. The above passage is actually a prophecy fulfilled by the first coming of our Lord and Savior Jesus Christ. God is now instructing His people to also forgive and to let no debt remain outstanding as stated by the below passage:

> Let *no debt remain outstanding*, except the continuing debt to love one another, for whoever loves others has fulfilled the law. (Romans 13:8–10 NIV, emphasis added)

We were completely forgiven—we were cleansed and purified by the blood of the Lamb. Let us now look at this wonderful New Testament story to see how the prophecy came to be fulfilled:

> Then Pilate took Jesus and had him flogged. The soldiers twisted together a crown of thorns and put it on his head. They clothed him in a *purple robe*. (John 19:1–3 NIV, emphasis added)

> Carrying his own *cross*, he went out to the place of the Skull (which in Aramaic is called Golgotha). (John 19:16–17 NIV, emphasis added)

> A jar of wine vinegar was there, so they soaked a sponge in it, put the sponge on a stalk of the *hyssop* plant, and lifted it to Jesus' lips. When he had received the drink, Jesus said, "It is finished." With that, he bowed his head and gave up his spirit. (John 19:28–30 NIV, emphasis added)

> Instead, one of the soldiers pierced Jesus' side with a spear, bringing a sudden flow of *blood* and *water* ... These things happened so that the scripture would be

fulfilled: "Not one of his bones will be broken." (John
19:31–37 NIV, emphasis added)

From the above passages, we can notice five elements that
were present during the crucifixion of the Lord Jesus: (1) the
wooden cross, (2) the stalk of hyssop, (3) the purple robe, (4)
the blood, and (5) the water.

What are these elements? Would there be any significance why
these elements were present during that momentous day? What
do these elements represent? To appreciate and understand this
story from the New Testament, we need to connect it to the
Old Testament.

Let us read the following passages:

> Cleanse me with *hyssop*, and I will be clean; wash me,
> and I will be whiter than snow. (Psalms 51:7 NIV,
> emphasis added)

> He shall *purify* the house with the bird's *blood*, the
> fresh *water*, the live bird, the *cedar wood*, the *hyssop* and
> the *scarlet yarn*. (Leviticus 14:49–52 NIV, emphasis
> added)

It is clear from the above passages that the five elements
mentioned in the New Testament were actually the required
elements used for cleansing and purifying during the time of
the Old Testament:

(1) The cedar wood corresponding to the wooden cross
    where the Lord Jesus was crucified
(2) The hyssop corresponding to the stalk where the
    sponge with wine vinegar was put to lift it to Jesus's lips

(3) The scarlet yarn corresponding to the purple robe worn by the Lord Jesus before He was crucified on the cross
(4) The blood of the bird corresponding to the blood of the Lord Jesus
(5) The fresh water corresponding to the water that flowed (along with the blood) from the Lord Jesus's side when pierced by one of the soldiers

These elements required for cleansing and purifying in the Old Testament were actually used by God to relay the prophecy of cleansing and purifying in the New Testament.

It is indeed a prophecy fulfilled—the five elements that were present when the Lord Jesus was crucified have brought a message of forgiveness for God's chosen people. We were already cleansed and purified, all our sins were forgiven, and the Lord's time for canceling debts has been proclaimed.

We will now see another prophecy fulfilled as a result of this message of forgiveness. As mentioned previously from scripture, the Lord Jesus's side was pierced, and not one of His bones was found broken.

From the side of our body, we can find our ribs, and this again reminds us of the story of Adam and Eve as narrated by the following passage:

> So the LORD God caused the man to fall into a deep sleep; and while he was sleeping, he took one of the man's ribs and then closed up the place with flesh. Then the LORD God made a woman from the rib he had taken out of the man, and he brought her to the man. (Genesis 2:21–24 NIV)

From this passage we can see that God took one of the man's ribs, which signifies that there is a broken or missing bone. The man is Adam, and from one of his ribs, the woman Eve was formed. As mentioned in chapter 8 of this book, the man, Adam, represents the Lord Jesus Christ, while the wife, Eve, represents the church (God's chosen people), and the prophecy states that the two shall become one. The broken or missing bone is a message of separation—Eve was separated from Adam. This represents that the church was actually one with the Lord Jesus before the beginning of time (from eternity past before the creation of the world) but was separated because of rebellion. Because of God's great mercy and unconditional love for us, He made a promise that the two shall again become one.

To fulfill this promise, He needed to make the supreme sacrifice so that our sins would be forgiven and all our debts would be cancelled.

To give emphasis to this supreme sacrifice, let us again read the following passage:

> For this reason *a man will leave his father* and mother and be united to his wife, and the two will become one flesh. (Ephesians 5:31 NIV, emphasis added)

God is one—this is the perfect union of God the Father, the Lord Jesus, and the Holy Spirit. In order to save His beloved chosen people, the Lord Jesus needed to die. And to die means He had to leave God the Father—the first and only moment in eternity that the perfect union was broken—an indescribable, unspeakable, and unimaginable scene that required the greatest sacrifice of all.

The Lord Jesus can never die if He is in union with the Source of life. At the cross He was stripped of His deity, and all His connections with God the Father were cut off. As a result, He suffered and died not only physically but also spiritually—He tasted the torments of hell for three days and three nights, as described by scripture saying: "For as Jonah was three days and three nights in the belly of a huge fish, so the Son of Man will be three days and three nights in the heart of the earth."

He was able to bear this supreme sacrifice (a man will leave his father) because it would result in the church being united with Him (and be united to his wife, and the two will become one flesh)—the fulfillment of the prophecy and of God's promise that was made before the beginning of time.

When the Lord Jesus died on the cross with all the elements required for cleansing and purification present, the LORD's time for canceling debts had been proclaimed. After that, there was no broken rib found when the Lord Jesus's side was pierced. This represents that because we are now completely forgiven, and the prophecy of becoming one (God and His chosen people) has now also been fulfilled. Our Lord and Savior Jesus Christ is most worthy of praise.

Let us read the following passage:

> This is the one who came by water and blood—Jesus Christ. He did not come by water only, but by water and blood. And it is the Spirit who testifies because the Spirit is the truth. For there are three that testify: the Spirit, the water and the blood; and the three are in agreement. (1 John 5:6–8 NIV)

CHAPTER 10

ONLY ONE PROPHECY

But this is how God fulfilled what he had foretold through
all the prophets, saying that his Messiah would suffer.
(Acts 3:18 NIV)

The journey of Abraham, Isaac, Jacob, and the nation Israel
can be summed up in seven major stages. All these stages
prophetically represent the journey of the Lord Jesus and
the church. And all whose names have been written in the
Lamb's Book of Life will take the same journey individually.
Let us find out these seven stages by looking at the story of a
man named Stephen. Before he was stoned to death, the Holy
Spirit empowered him to deliver a concise, undeniable speech
narrating the journey of God's people and pointing to the Lord
Jesus as the coming Savior. Let us read the following passage:

> Now Stephen, *a man full of God's grace and power*,
> performed great wonders and signs among the people.
> Opposition arose, however, from members of the
> Synagogue of the Freedmen (as it was called)—Jews
> of Cyrene and Alexandria as well as the provinces of
> Cilicia and Asia—who began to argue with Stephen.
> But they could not stand up against *the wisdom the*

Spirit gave him as he spoke. (Acts 6:8–15 NIV, emphasis added)

After the Lord Jesus rose from the dead, He spent another forty days with His disciples. Within these forty days, He taught them more about the kingdom of God and told them that the work the Father had given Him for that time being had already been accomplished and that for a while He needed to leave and go back to the Father. But He promised them that He would come back and would not leave them orphans, so He had prepared their hearts for the coming of the Holy Spirit.

This is in accordance with God's perfect plan of salvation (the fulfillment of the Eternal Covenant):

(1) The church will first become one with the Holy Spirit (while inside of time).
(2) The church, being one with the Holy Spirit, will become one with the Lord Jesus at His Second Coming (at the ending of time).
(3) The church, being one with the Holy Spirit and the Lord Jesus, will become one with God the Father (in eternity future).

Since we are still inside of time, it follows that the Holy Spirit will be our Guide, our Teacher, our Friend, our Counselor, and the Life and Power of the church. While inside of time, God's chosen people (whose names have been written in the Lamb's Book of Life) are all connected to the Father and the Lord Jesus because of the Holy Spirit.

In the book of Acts, the disciples of the Lord Jesus are always introduced individually with the following description: "a man full of the Holy Spirit" or "a man full of God's grace and power." With this description comes the performance of great wonders and signs and healings and miracles.

Stephen belonged to this description, and no one could stand up against the wisdom the Holy Spirit gave him. In those days he was accused of speaking against the Law. To his defense, he delivered a speech about what the Law stated regarding the journey of God's people and proved that Christ was the culmination of the Law. This speech was recorded in the seventh chapter of the book of Acts, and from this speech we derive the seven major stages of the journey of Israel, representing the prophetic journey of the Lord Jesus and the church:

(1) Stage 1: To the land of Canaan (the Canaan stage)
(2) Stage 2: To the land of Egypt (the Egypt stage)
(3) Stage 3: To the wilderness (the wilderness stage)
(4) Stage 4: To the Promised Land (the Jerusalem stage)
(5) Stage 5: To the land of Babylon (the Babylon stage)
(6) Stage 6: Restoration of the temple (the New Jerusalem)
(7) Stage 7: Years of silence (the First Coming of Jesus)

Stages 5 and 6 were emphasized by the following passages:

> But because our ancestors angered the God of heaven, he gave them into the hands of Nebuchadnezzar the Chaldean, king of Babylon, who destroyed this temple and *deported the people to Babylon*. (Ezra 5:12 NIV, emphasis added)

> However, in the first year of Cyrus king of Babylon, King Cyrus issued a decree to *rebuild this house of God*. (Ezra 5:13–15 NIV, emphasis added)

Stage 7 (last stage) was an age of great trouble with the many historical rises and falls of the nation Israel, including the desolation of the temple at Jerusalem.

We will now compare the stages of the journey of Israel with the stages of the journey of the Lord Jesus and the church:

(1) Abraham lived in the land of Canaan, where Isaac was born. From Isaac came Jacob, who became the father of the twelve patriarchs (the nation Israel).
   • The Lord Jesus was born in this land (the First Coming).

(2) Jacob and all his family went to live in the land of Egypt.
   • The Lord Jesus lived in the land of Egypt.

(3) The nation Israel passed through the wilderness on its way to the Promised Land.
   • The Lord Jesus was baptized and was tempted in the wilderness.

(4) The nation Israel entered and conquered the land of Canaan (the Promised Land).
   • The Lord Jesus died and rose again in this land, after which the church was born.

(5) The nation Israel was conquered and was exiled to the land of Babylon.
   • The church gets inside Babylon (our present time).

(6) The nation Israel came out of Babylon and restored the temple at Jerusalem.

- The church will come out of Babylon and will enter the New Jerusalem.

(7) There were years of silence, after which came the Messiah (First Coming of the Lord Jesus).
- This is the fulfillment of the Second Coming of the Lord Jesus.

We will now look at each of these stages and realize that each has a representation that has something to do with the two covenants as well as with the events that took place in eternity past (before the beginning of time). Let us emphasize that at the seventh stage, there were four hundred years of silence, and at the end of it, the First Coming of the Lord Jesus took place. This signaled the start of the fulfillment of each prophetic stage of the journey.

Stage 1: To the Land of Canaan
The Birth of Jesus in the Town of David

Isaac was born in this land. This stage is a prophecy about the Lord Jesus to be born in this land as stated by this passage:

> So Joseph also went up from the town of Nazareth in Galilee to Judea, *to Bethlehem the town of David*, because he belonged to the house and line of David … While they were there, the time came for the baby to be born, and she gave birth to her firstborn, a son. She wrapped him in cloths and *placed him in a manger*, because *there was no guest room available for them*. (Luke 2:1–7 NIV, emphasis added)

God promised Abraham that he and his descendants after him would possess the land, but at that time He gave him no inheritance there, not even enough ground to set his foot on. In the same way, the Lord Jesus was born in this same land, and He is the Heir of all things (seen and unseen). But He was placed in a manger because no room was available for His parents.

The land of Canaan was supposed to be the Promised Land, a beautiful land flowing with milk and honey. This represents the original intention of our Creator—for us to be heirs of His kingdom and His corulers of all His vast creations. However, something happened in eternity past—a deception occurred, and God's people were misdirected, causing the delay of inheritance. This is also the first conflict as mentioned in chapters 2 and 3.

Stage 1 Representation: From eternity past and before the beginning of time, the New Covenant (Eternal Covenant) is our inheritance but was delayed because of the Old Covenant.

Stage 2: To the Land of Egypt
The Escape to Egypt

As stated by scripture, the time had not yet come to possess the land because Israel needed first to take another stage of the journey—to Egypt. This stage is actually a prophecy about the Lord Jesus going to Egypt and living there for some time, as stated by the following passage:

> When they had gone, an angel of the Lord appeared to Joseph in a dream. "Get up," he said, "take the child and his mother and *escape to Egypt*" … And so was fulfilled what the Lord had said through the prophet: "*Out of Egypt I called my son*." (Matthew 2:13–15 NIV, emphasis added)

Egypt represents the world, the beginning until the ending of time. This is the inside of time, where all the days were declared evil—there is oppression, adversity, suffering, pain, and slavery to worldliness and human traditions. But this is also the way of escape and part of the fulfillment of the plan of God for the salvation of His people.

Scripture states that the descendants of Abraham will be strangers in a country not their own, and they will be enslaved and mistreated. In the same way, God's chosen people were enslaved to worldliness and human traditions. But just as God has called out His Son out of Egypt, He has called out His people, and He is leading them to the land of their inheritance.

Stage 2 Representation: We were born into the world—inside of time—under the Law, bound to disobedience and have once became slave to worldliness and human traditions.

Stage 3: To the Wilderness
Jesus Tested in the Wilderness

Then again, Israel came out of Egypt but did not go straight to the Promised Land—they passed through the wilderness where they received the Law (the Old Covenant). This is the third stage of the journey we must take, and we must realize that God is sending us a message—a representation of what really happened in eternity past.

Israel passing through the wilderness and staying there for forty years is a prophecy about the Lord Jesus. After his baptism He was led into the wilderness, as narrated by the following passage:

> Then Jesus was led by the Spirit *into the wilderness* to
> be tempted by the devil. After fasting forty days and
> forty nights, he was hungry. The tempter came to him
> and said, "If you are the Son of God, tell these stones
> to become bread." Jesus answered, "It is written: 'Man
> shall not live on bread alone, but on every word that
> comes from the mouth of God.'" (Matthew 4:1–11
> NIV, emphasis added)

Israel came out of Egypt and could have reached the Promised
Land in a few days. But why did the people pass through the
wilderness and wander there for forty years? During those
years the Law was introduced to them, but instead of the
Law doing them good, the majority of them died in the
wilderness.

Scripture states that in the wilderness, the people of Israel
refused to obey God. Instead, they rejected Him and, in their
hearts, turned back to Egypt. They told Aaron, "Make us gods
who will go before us. As for this fellow Moses who led us out
of Egypt—we don't know what has happened to him!" That
was the time they made an idol in the form of a calf.

They died because in their hearts they turned back to Egypt.
This means that they combined the Old Covenant teaching
with human traditions (refer to chapter 3, teaching 3). This
is also the second conflict, as mentioned in chapters 2 and 3.

Those whose hearts were set to follow purely the Law knew
that they couldn't really obey it and had realized their real
need—the New and Everlasting Covenant. Notice that after
forty years in the wilderness, only their children (and only
two adults, Caleb and Joshua) were able to enter the Promised
Land. Not even Moses was able to enter, although he pleaded

with God. To enter the Promised Land means to enter the New Covenant (get out of the Old Covenant). God wanted to send us a prophetic message, so He did not allow Moses to enter the Promised Land (for the Law was given through Moses).

Moses was greatly used to deliver the people of Israel from their slavery under Egypt and also to guide them to the Promised Land. In the same way, the Law (Old Covenant) was used for us to be free from worldliness and human traditions as well as to guide us into the New and Everlasting Covenant. But just as Moses was not able to enter the Promised Land, we also cannot bring the Law along with us if we are to enter God's kingdom.

Notice that in the wilderness, the devil tempted the Lord Jesus by using the Law (the Old Covenant). The Lord Jesus resisted the devil by using the New Covenant (word that comes from the mouth of God). We were able to enter God's kingdom after hearing and believing the gospel (the New and Everlasting Covenant—the word that comes from the mouth of God). The Lord Jesus is the Word, who was from the beginning (from eternity) and was with God and was God and was made flesh.

Before entering the Promised Land, Israel had to pass through the river Jordan. This is the baptism of repentance, which means that they had to die from the Old Covenant and then live to the New Covenant.

The Lord Jesus was also baptized from the same river, after which He heard the Father say to Him, "This is my beloved Son, with whom I am well pleased." This is the same confirmation the Father gives to all who have been released from the Law so that they serve in the new way of the Spirit, not in the old way of the written code.

Stage 3 Representation: The Old Covenant or the Law was used to lead us to the New Covenant but was delayed because of mixture with human traditions.

Stage 4: To the Promised Land
At the Cross—the Birth of the Church

Upon entering the Promised Land, God's people had to face their enemies in battle, but God gave them sure victory until Israel was firmly established. And at the time of King David and King Solomon, Israel became great and powerful, so much so that almost all nations became subject to its kingdom.

Israel conquering the Promised Land is a prophecy about the Lord Jesus giving the victory shout for the birth of the church, as stated by the following passages:

> Jesus said, "It is finished." With that, he bowed his head and gave up his spirit. (John 19:28–30 NIV)

> But now, by dying to what once bound us, we have been released from the Law so that we serve in the new way of the Spirit, and not in the old way of the written code. (Romans 7:4–6 NIV)

While the Lord Jesus was crucified and about to die, He declared the victory statement "It is finished." His death is the key to the birth of the New Covenant people (the church). After three days He rose again and stayed with His disciples a few more days. Then He bid them a temporary farewell and was taken to the heavens to give way for the first stage of the fulfillment of the New Covenant—the coming of the promised Holy Spirit who is the Life and Power of the church.

After that, the church became great and powerful—delivering the New Covenant message to all nations, accompanied with works of miracles, wonders, and healings through the help and guidance of the Holy Spirit.

Stage 4 Representation: We were able to enter into the New Covenant because of the supreme sacrifice of our Lord and Savior Jesus Christ.

Stage 5: To the Land of Babylon
The Church Inside of Babylon

But then again there was the fifth stage of the journey, which is another representation of what really happened in eternity past. Israel was exiled to Babylon, which is a prophecy about the church combining the New Covenant teaching with the Old Covenant teaching (refer to chapter 3, teaching 4). The Lord Jesus has given instruction to His people to come out of Babylon as stated by this passage:

> Come out of her, my people, so that you will not share in her sins, so that you will not receive any of her plagues. (Revelation 18:4 NIV)

Babylon came from the root word *Babel* which means "to confuse" or "to mix," as in the accounts of the Tower of Babel, where God confused the language of the whole world.

Daniel and his friends kept themselves pure during their exile in Babylon. They ate only vegetables and never ate meat from the king's table. To eat from the king's table means to be one with the king of Babylon, which further means to partake of another teaching aside from the teaching they already have. Babylon is the combining of the New Covenant teaching with the Old Covenant teaching, and the church is now under this confusion but without even noticing it.

This is the final conflict in the church, which will soon be resolved before the Second Coming of our Lord Jesus Christ. The only instruction the Lord Jesus has given the church before His Second Coming is to come out of this conflict, and then God will destroy Babylon and will lead His people to the New Jerusalem so that God's temple will be restored.

Stage 5 Representation: We were deceived to mix New Covenant teaching with Old Covenant teaching or with human traditions rendering the church powerless.

Stage 6: Restoration of the Temple (New Jerusalem)
Complete Unity in the Last Days

Israel coming out of Babylon and going back to the Promised Land to restore the temple at Jerusalem is a prophecy about the church being united, as stated by the following passages:

> They will be my people, and I will be their God. I will give them *singleness of heart and action*. (Jeremiah 32:38–39 NIV, emphasis added)

> All the believers were one in heart and mind. (Acts 4:32–34 NIV)

Our God is one. Before the Second Coming of our Lord Jesus, the church must be in the right position spiritually, which means that there must be unity for all the believers.

For the church to be one, there must be only one teaching—the New and Everlasting Covenant teaching. To do this the church must first come out of Babylon (mixture of the New Covenant teaching with the Old Covenant teaching and human traditions).

We cannot preach the gospel as a testimony if we proclaim that our God is one yet we are not one in heart and in action. Unity means we are many yet we are one. We were created after God's own image, after His own likeness. There is the Father, there is Jesus, and there is the Holy Spirit—three distinct persons yet together as one—the perfect picture of the perfect unity.

The message of the cross is about unity. The main reason God created us is to be one with Him. Because of sin we were separated from God. The Lord Jesus took to Himself the penalty for our sin—He died on the cross. By hearing and believing this gospel, we can now go to God and again be one with Him.

By complete unity in the Last Days, God will place His people in the right position spiritually—as promised by God, prayed for by the Lord Jesus, and powered by the Holy Spirit. This we will discuss further in the concluding chapters.

Stage 6 Representation: We will come out of the final conflict and the church will unite as one having only one teaching—the New and Everlasting Covenant teaching.

Stage 7: The Day of God's Wrath and Judgment (Years of Silence)
The Second Coming of the Lord Jesus

The destruction of Babylon after the nation Israel came out is a prophecy about the day of God's wrath and judgment, as stated by the following passage:

> See, the day of the Lord is coming—a cruel day, with
> wrath and fierce anger—to make the land desolate and
> destroy the sinners within it. (Isaiah 13:9 NIV)

Once the church comes out of Babylon, she will enter New
Jerusalem and will now be ready for the Second Coming. The
Lord Jesus will now take the church with Him to give way for
the second stage of the fulfillment of the Eternal Covenant—
the promised wedding of the Lamb. This is where the chosen
people (the church), who are one with the Holy Spirit, will
become one with God the Son (the Lord Jesus). Those who
were left behind will face God's wrath and judgment (those
whose names were not written in the Lamb's Book of Life).
This is the final stage of the journey. After this comes the
final stage of the fulfillment of the eternal gospel—the stage
where those who are one with the Holy Spirit and the Lord
Jesus will become one with God the Father. Thus the Eternal
Covenant will be fulfilled, and all will become one with God
because God is one.

Stage 7 Representation: This is where God's wrath and
judgment will be poured out to those who will remain inside
the Old Covenant as well as the fulfillment of the Second
Coming of the Lord Jesus for the sake of the New and
Everlasting Covenant people.

The Three Major Conflicts as Prophesied After the Flood:
The Sons of Noah

To further emphasize these major stages of the one journey, we
need to take a deeper look into the accounts of Noah's sons,
especially of his son Ham and his descendants. After the flood,
evil should have been completely eradicated, and all who were
to come out of the ark were supposed to be righteous people.

But why would one son and his descendants end up as evil, rebellious people?

This again happened for a purpose. Everything was so well arranged by God to relay the message of the eternal gospel—a shadow representation of what really happened in eternity past.

Let us read the following passages:

> When Noah awoke from his wine and found out what his youngest son had done to him, he said, "Cursed be Canaan! The lowest of slaves will he be to his brothers." He also said, "Praise be to the LORD, the God of Shem! May Canaan be the slave of Shem. May God extend Japheth's territory; *may Japheth live in the tents of Shem*, and may Canaan be the slave of Japheth." (Genesis 9:18–27 NIV, emphasis added)

> The sons of Ham: Cush, Egypt, Put and Canaan. The sons of Cush: Seba, Havilah, Sabta, Raamah and Sabteka. The sons of Raamah: Sheba and Dedan. *Cush* was the father of Nimrod, who became a mighty warrior on earth. *Egypt* was the father of the Ludites, Anamites, Lehabites, Naphtuhites, Pathrusites, Kasluhites (from whom the Philistines came) and Caphtorites. *Canaan* was the father of Sidon his firstborn, and of the Hittites, Jebusites, Amorites, Girgashites, Hivites, Arkites, Sinites, Arvadites, Zemarites and Hamathites. (1 Chronicles 1:8–16 NIV, emphasis added)

It is clear from the above passages that the stages mentioned for the one journey we have to take were firmly determined and established by God. These were also the three conflicts as mentioned in chapters 2 and 3 of this book—they have been prophesied even from the time of Noah.

Notice the following:

(1) The two blessed sons of Noah (Shem and Japheth) were to unite as one family (may Japheth live in the tents of Shem). This represents the nation Israel as well as the church (God's beloved chosen people, whose names were written in the Lamb's Book of Life).

(2) The sons of Ham and their descendants were cursed:

(a) Canaan—the father of Sidon, his firstborn, and of the Hittites, Jebusites, Amorites, Girgashites, Hivites, Arkites, Sinites, Arvadites, Zemarites, and Hamathites.

These were the nations whose lands were conquered by Israel. This represents the Promised Land, which is the inheritance of Israel but was first occupied by the Canaanites—the first conflict. Israel had to leave first this land and settle temporarily in the land of Egypt. The Lord Jesus was born in the land of Canaan but also had to leave His birthplace to go to the land of Egypt. This is also a representation of our journey before going to the land of our inheritance; the New Covenant (tree of life) is our inheritance but was delayed because the Old Covenant (tree of the knowledge of good and evil) came to the picture. From eternity past we have rejected the Eternal Covenant and chosen another covenant—this is the Canaan conflict before the beginning of time.

(b) Egypt—the father of the Ludites, Anamites, Lehabites, Naphtuhites, Pathrusites, Kasluhites (from whom the Philistines came), and Caphtorites.

The people of Israel were enslaved for so many years in the land of Egypt, so before coming back to the Promised Land, they needed to pass through the wilderness, where many died because their hearts were inclined to go back to Egypt—the second conflict. This is a representation of the combining of the Old Covenant teaching with human traditions (teaching 3, as discussed in chapter 3). We were once slaves to worldliness and human traditions, and combining this with the Old Covenant would result in numerous world religions—this is the Egypt conflict that has been happening inside of time.

(c) Cush—the father of Nimrod, who became a mighty warrior on earth. Nimrod was the founder of Babylon—the land where the nation Israel was taken into captivity.

After slavery from Egypt and passing through the wilderness, Israel conquered the land of the Canaanites and established itself in the Promised Land. But after some time, Israel was conquered by Babylon and was sent into exile—the third and final conflict. This represents the current time in church history, where there is confusion (a mixture of the New Covenant teaching with the Old Covenant teaching), which results in numerous church denominations—this is the Babylon conflict before the ending of time (Last Days).

The Second Coming of our Lord and Savior Jesus Christ is now very near. Babylon is about to be destroyed; the church will come out of Babylon and will enter New Jerusalem.

We will discuss more about this prophecy in the next chapter and learn that our God is indeed almighty and full of wisdom.

To summarize, the seven stages of the one journey we have to take are the following:

(1) The Canaan Stage
     Representation: From eternity past and before the beginning of time, the New Covenant is our inheritance but was delayed because of the Old Covenant.

(2) The Egypt Stage
     Representation: We were born into the world—inside of time—under the Law, bound to disobedience and have once became slave to worldliness and human traditions.

(3) The Wilderness Stage
     Representation: The Old Covenant or the Law was used to lead us to the New Covenant but was delayed because of mixture with human traditions.

(4) The Jerusalem Stage
     Representation: We were able to enter into the New Covenant because of the supreme sacrifice of our Lord and Savior Jesus Christ.

(5) The Babylon Stage
     Representation: We were deceived to mix New Covenant teaching with Old Covenant teaching

or with human traditions, rendering the church powerless.

(6) The New Jerusalem Stage
Representation: We will come out of the final conflict and the church will unite as one having only one teaching.

(7) The Years of Silence Stage (the First Coming of Jesus)
Representation: This is where God's wrath and judgment will be poured out to those who will remain inside the Old Covenant as well as the fulfillment of the Second Coming.

There is indeed only one prophecy and only one journey to take. Great and awesome is the wisdom of our God.

CHAPTER 11

FALL OF BABYLON AND RISE OF NEW JERUSALEM

Come out of her, my people, so that you will not share in
her sins, so that you will not receive any of her plagues.
(Revelation 18:4 NIV)

The purpose of this chapter is not to discuss the book of
Revelation in detail but to highlight the main topics and allow
us to discover that scripture has only one simple message—the
fulfillment of the two covenants that has something to do with
Babylon and the New Jerusalem. This will help us realize that
there is, in reality, only one instruction that was given to the
church before the Second Coming.

Israel is the representation of the church, which means that
all prophecies proclaimed and fulfilled for Israel were also
proclaimed and will be fulfilled for the church. To emphasize,
these are the prophecies with double fulfillment—just as the
prophecy of the coming of the Messiah will be fulfilled twice.
The first was to fulfill the Old Covenant for the sake of Israel,
and the second would be to fulfill the New Covenant for the
sake of the church.

The same goes with the prophecies concerning Babylon and the New Jerusalem. And these prophecies are in line with the seven major stages of the one journey we have to take and the three conflicts mentioned from the previous chapters. The Old Covenant was fulfilled and has become obsolete, but the New Covenant once fulfilled will continue forever because it is an Everlasting Covenant.

Let us look further at the scripture and uncover the prophecies concerning Babylon and the New Jerusalem. From the Old Testament we can find the following passages:

> Babylon has fallen, has fallen! All the images of its gods lie shattered on the ground! (Isaiah 21:9 NIV)

> Leave Babylon, flee from the Babylonians! (Isaiah 48:20 NIV)

> Flee out of Babylon; Leave the land of the Babylonian. (Jeremiah 50:8 NIV)

> Flee from Babylon! Run for your lives! Do not be destroyed because of her sins. (Jeremiah 51:6 NIV)

> "Before your eyes I will repay Babylon and all who live in Babylonia for all the wrong they have done in Zion," declares the Lord. (Jeremiah 51:24 NIV)

> Come out of her, my people! Run for your lives! Run from the fierce anger of the Lord. (Jeremiah 51:45 NIV)

> Babylon must fall because of Israel's slain, just as the slain in all the earth have fallen because of Babylon. (Jeremiah 51:49 NIV)

> For you this whole vision is nothing but words sealed in a scroll. (Isaiah 29:11 NIV)

These Old Testament prophecies were already declared and fulfilled thousands of years ago, but during those times they only referred to the coming salvation of the nation Israel from the hands of the Babylonians.

Because the church was yet unknown during those times, there is no way that these prophecies can be understood as referring to the church. This is why the prophet Isaiah wrote: "These are nothing but words sealed in a scroll." Ultimately, these prophecies not only referred to the nation Israel but also to the church and were reserved for these very Last Days.

Notice the similarities of the abovementioned Old Testament passages and the below New Testament passages that were taken from the last book of the Bible (book of Revelation):

> Do not seal up the words of the prophecy of this book, because the time is near. (Revelation 22:10 NIV)

> Fallen! Fallen is Babylon the Great, which made all the nations drink the maddening wine of her adulteries. (Revelation 14:8 NIV)

> God remembered Babylon the Great and gave her the cup filled with the wine of the fury of his wrath. (Revelation 16:19 NIV)

> This title was written on her forehead: MYSTERY BABYLON THE GREAT THE MOTHER OF PROSTITUTES AND OF THE ABOMINATIONS OF THE EARTH ... In her was found the blood of

prophets and of the saints, and of all who have been killed on the earth. (Revelation 17:5; 18:24 NIV)

Come out of her, my people, so that you will not share in her sins, so that you will not receive any of her plagues. (Revelation 18:4 NIV)

Many Old Testament prophecies with reference to Babylon were again mentioned in the Book of Revelation, although they already had their fulfillment when the nation Israel came out of Babylon and restored the temple at Jerusalem. We can safely conclude that these prophecies have not only one fulfillment but also two—one for Israel and one for the church. To help us further, let us again emphasize these points:

(1) A land of inheritance was promised to Israel but was delayed because of the Canaanites.

The New Covenant is the true inheritance of the church but was delayed because of the Old Covenant. Likewise, God's intention for us is to partake of the tree of life, but we have chosen to partake of the tree of the knowledge of good and evil. This represents that all of mankind from eternity past (before the beginning of time) has rejected the Eternal Covenant and has rebelled against God as Creator by choosing another covenant. This is the Canaan conflict.

(2) Because of the Canaan conflict, Israel had to go and stay in Egypt and was enslaved there for so many years. When it was time for its people to go back to the land of their inheritance, again they were delayed. They needed to pass through the wilderness because their hearts were inclined to go back to Egypt.

The Old Covenant was used to lead the people to the New Covenant, but because the former was contaminated with human traditions, many were not able to enter the latter. Wilderness represents the stage were many have fallen because of the mixture of Old Covenant teaching with human traditions, which resulted in the birth of numerous world religions. The church was able to escape the wilderness because, for a time, her heart was not inclined to the world (inside of time), thus she was able to enter the New Covenant.

Those who have not escaped (those whose names were not written in the Lamb's Book of Life) have fallen because of the Egypt conflict.

(3) Because of the Babylonians, the temple at Jerusalem was destroyed, and Israel was forced out of its inheritance and was exiled for so many years inside Babylon. Following the exile, Israel came out of Babylon and got back to Jerusalem, restoring the temple. But the heart of Israel was inclined to Babylon (resulting in the birth of different Jewish denominations like the Pharisees and Sadducees), so God's wrath and judgment were poured out. There were years of silence, but after that came the fulfillment of the first coming of the Messiah.

This is the stage where the church became powerless because New Covenant teaching was contaminated with Old Covenant teaching or with human traditions, which resulted in the birth of numerous church denominations.

This is the Babylon conflict (before the ending of time) which this chapter emphasizes.

The church will come out of Babylon because the Holy Spirit will lead her to victory toward New Jerusalem. But those who will not come out (those whose names were not written in the Lamb's Book of Life) will be judged and be destroyed along with Babylon, which will mark the fulfillment of the Second Coming of our King. As mentioned in the beginning of this chapter and to give further emphasis, the major topics of the book of Revelation (last book of the Bible) always point to Babylon and the New Jerusalem. Let us now see these major topics in general:

(1) Warnings to the Seven Churches
(2) The Scroll Sealed with Seven Seals
(3) The Seven Trumpets
(4) The Seven Bowls
(5) Fall of Babylon and Rise of New Jerusalem

Warnings to the Seven Churches

The first major topic of the book of Revelation is about the warnings and comments to the seven churches. Let us read the following passage:

> Write on a scroll what you see and send it to the seven churches: to Ephesus, Smyrna, Pergamum, Thyatira, Sardis, Philadelphia and Laodicea. (Revelation 1:11 NIV)

(1) To the angel of the church in Ephesus ...
     Negative comment: "You have forsaken your first love."

(2) To the angel of the church in Smyrna ...
     No negative comment.

(3) To the angel of the church in Pergamum ...
     Negative comment: "You hold to the teaching of Balaam" and "You hold to the teaching of the Nicolaitans."

(4) To the angel of the church in Thyatira ...
     Negative comment: "You hold to the teaching of Jezebel."

(5) To the angel of the church in Sardis ...
     Negative comment: "You have a reputation of being alive but you are dead."

(6) To the angel of the church in Philadelphia ...
     No negative comment.

(7) To the angel of the church in Laodicea ...
     Negative comment: "You are neither hot nor cold."

All these negative comments to the five out of seven churches of ancient Asia Minor refer to Babylon (again, Babylon came from the root word *Babel*, which means "to confuse" or "to mix"). This is the Babylon stage, as discussed in chapter 10, and the serpent's "did God really say" teaching, as discussed in chapter 3. This is also the Babylon conflict, which is the third and final conflict in the church, as discussed in chapter 2 and the very message discussed in chapter 1. Let us now proceed with the next major topic.

The Scroll Sealed with Seven Seals

The second major topic of the book of Revelation is about the scroll with seven seals. Let us read the following passage:

Then I saw in the right hand of him who sat on the throne a scroll with writing on both sides and sealed with seven seals ... Then one of the elders said to me, "Do not weep! See, the Lion of the tribe of Judah, the Root of David, has triumphed. He is able to open the scroll and its seven seals." (Revelation 5:1–5 NIV)

(1) The Lamb opened the first seal ...
Event: "There was a white horse; its rider held a bow, and he was given a crown, and he rode out as a conqueror bent on conquest."

(2) The Lamb opened the second seal ...
Event: "Another horse came out, a fiery red one; its rider was given power to take peace from the earth and to make people kill each other; to him was given a large sword."

(3) The Lamb opened the third seal ...
Event: "There was a black horse; its rider was holding a pair of scales in his hand."

(4) The Lamb opened the fourth seal ...
Event: "There was a pale horse; its rider was named Death, and Hades was following close behind him; they were given power over a fourth of the earth to kill by sword, famine and plague, and by the wild beasts of the earth."

(5) The Lamb opened the fifth seal ...
Event: "There were under the altar the souls of those who had been slain because of the word of God and the testimony they had maintained; then each of them was given a white robe, and they were told to wait a little

longer, until the full number of their fellow servants, their brothers and sisters, were killed just as they had been."

(6) The Lamb opened the sixth seal …
     Event: "There was a great earthquake; the sun turned black like sackcloth made of goat hair, the whole moon turned blood red, and the stars in the sky fell to earth, as figs drop from a fig tree when shaken by a strong wind; the heavens receded like a scroll being rolled up, and every mountain and island was removed from its place."

(7) The Lamb opened the seventh seal …
     Event: "There was silence in heaven for about half an hour; and then seven trumpets were given to the seven angels who stand before God."

Notice that every time a seal was opened, a great event would take place. Notice also that it is only the Lord Jesus who can open the seals, which means that God absolutely is in control.

When the seventh seal was opened, the seven trumpets were mentioned, which leads us to the next major topic.

The Seven Trumpets

The third major topic of the book of Revelation is about the seven trumpets. Let us read the following passage:

> When he opened the seventh seal, there was silence in heaven for about half an hour. And I saw the seven angels who stand before God, and to them were given seven trumpets. (Revelation 8:1–2 NIV)

(1) The first angel sounded his trumpet …
Event: "There came hail and fire mixed with blood, and it was hurled down on the earth; a third of the earth was burned up, a third of the trees were burned up, and all the green grass was burned up."

(2) The second angel sounded his trumpet …
Event: "Something like a huge mountain, all ablaze, was thrown into the sea; a third of the sea turned into blood, a third of the living creatures in the sea died, and a third of the ships were destroyed."

(3) The third angel sounded his trumpet …
Event: "A great star, blazing like a torch, fell from the sky on a third of the rivers and on the springs of water—the name of the star is Wormwood; a third of the waters turned bitter, and many people died from the waters that had become bitter."

(4) The fourth angel sounded his trumpet …
Event: "And a third of the sun was struck, a third of the moon, and a third of the stars, so that a third of them turned dark; a third of the day was without light, and also a third of the night."

(5) The fifth angel sounded his trumpet …
Event: "There was a star that had fallen from the sky to the earth; the star was given the key to the shaft of the Abyss; when he opened the Abyss, smoke rose from it like the smoke from a gigantic furnace; the sun and sky were darkened by the smoke from the Abyss; and out of the smoke locusts came down on the earth and were given power like that of scorpions of the earth; they were told not to harm the grass of the earth or

any plant or tree, but only those people who did not have the seal of God on their foreheads; they were not allowed to kill them but only to torture them for five months."

(6) The sixth angel sounded his trumpet ...
Event: "There was a voice coming from the four horns of the golden altar that is before God; it said to the sixth angel who had the trumpet, 'Release the four angels who are bound at the great river Euphrates.' And the four angels who had been kept ready for this very hour and day and month and year were released to kill a third of mankind."

(7) The seventh angel sounded his trumpet ...
Event: "There were loud voices in heaven, which said: 'The kingdom of the world has become the kingdom of our Lord and of his Messiah, and he will reign for ever and ever.' ... then God's temple in heaven was opened, and within his temple was seen the ark of his covenant; and there came flashes of lightning, rumblings, peals of thunder, an earthquake and a severe hailstorm."

After the seventh angel sounded his trumpet, the following were also mentioned:

(a) The woman and the dragon
(b) The beast out of the sea
(c) The beast out of the earth
(d) The Lamb and the 144,000
(e) The three angels
(f) Harvesting the earth and trampling the winepress

Again, notice that every time a trumpet was sounded, great events would take place and prove that God was indeed in control. After the seven seals were all opened and the seven trumpets were all sounded, Babylon was again mentioned, as stated by the following passage:

> A second angel followed and said, "Fallen! Fallen is Babylon the Great, which made all the nations drink the maddening wine of her adulteries." (Revelation 14:8 NIV)

When the seventh trumpet was sounded, seven angels were given seven golden bowls filled with the wrath of God. These are the seven last plagues—last because with them, God's wrath is completed. This leads us to the next major topic.

The Seven Bowls

The fourth major topic of the book of Revelation is about the seven bowls. Let us read the following passage:

> Then I heard a loud voice from the temple saying to the seven angels, "Go, pour out the seven bowls of God's wrath on the earth." (Revelation 16:1 NIV)

(1) The first angel poured out his bowl …
    Event: "The first bowl was poured out on the land, and ugly, festering sores broke out on the people who had the mark of the beast and worshiped its image."

(2) The second angel poured out his bowl …
    Event: "The second bowl was poured out on the sea, and it turned into blood like that of a dead person, and every living thing in the sea died."

(3) The third angel poured out his bowl …
Event: "The third bowl was poured out on the rivers and springs of water, and they became blood."

(4) The fourth angel poured out his bowl …
Event: "The fourth bowl was poured out on the sun, and the sun was allowed to scorch people with fire. They were seared by the intense heat and they cursed the name of God, who had control over these plagues, but they refused to repent and glorify him."

(5) The fifth angel poured out his bowl …
Event: "The fifth bowl was poured out on the throne of the beast, and its kingdom was plunged into darkness: people gnawed their tongues in agony and cursed the God of heaven because of their pains and their sores, but they refused to repent of what they had done."

(6) The sixth angel poured out his bowl …
Event: "The sixth bowl was poured out on the great river Euphrates, and its water was dried up to prepare the way for the kings from the East; there were three impure spirits that looked like frogs; they came out of the mouth of the dragon, out of the mouth of the beast and out of the mouth of the false prophet; they are demonic spirits that perform signs, and they go out to the kings of the whole world, to gather them for the battle on the great day of God Almighty."

(7) The seventh angel poured out his bowl …
Event: "The seventh bowl was poured out on into the air, and out of the temple came a loud voice from the throne, saying, "It is done!;" then there came flashes of lightning, rumblings, peals of thunder and a severe earthquake; no

earthquake like it has ever occurred since mankind has been on earth, so tremendous was the quake."

After the seven angels had finished pouring out the seven bowls, God's wrath was also completely poured out. Following all these events, Babylon was again mentioned:

> The great city split into three parts, and the cities of the nations collapsed. God remembered *Babylon* the Great and gave her the cup filled with the wine of the fury of his wrath. (Revelation 16:19 NIV, emphasis added)

Fall of Babylon and Rise of New Jerusalem

The fifth and last major topic of the book of Revelation is about the fall of Babylon and the rise of the New Jerusalem. Let us read the following passage:

> This title was written on her forehead: MYSTERY BABYLON THE GREAT THE MOTHER OF PROSTITUTES AND OF THE ABOMINATIONS OF THE EARTH ... In her was found the blood of prophets and of the saints, and of all who have been killed on the earth. (Revelation 17:5; 18:24 NIV)

Three chapters of the book of Revelation (chapters 17, 18, and 19) were specifically dedicated to narrating the judgment and the imminent complete destruction of Babylon. Once again, the only instruction the Lord Jesus has given the church before His Second Coming is to come out of Babylon (this is the end of the final conflict):

> Then I heard another voice from heaven say: "Come out of her, my people, so that you will not share in her

sins, so that you will not receive any of her plagues."
(Revelation 18:4 NIV)

Once the church comes out of Babylon, she will then enter the
New Jerusalem. The last three chapters of the last book of the
Bible were specifically dedicated to discussing the imminent
and most awaited coming of the New Jerusalem.

> I saw the Holy City, the new Jerusalem, coming down
> out of heaven from God, prepared as a bride beautifully
> dressed for her husband. And I heard a loud voice from
> the throne saying, "Now the dwelling of God is with
> men, and he will live with them. *They will be his people,
> and God himself will be with them and be their God."*
> (Revelation 21:2–3 NIV, emphasis added)

> This is the covenant I will make with the house of
> Israel after that time, declares the Lord. I will put my
> laws in their minds and write them on their hearts. *I
> will be their God, and they will be my people.* (Hebrews
> 8:7–13 NIV, emphasis added)

With regards the New Jerusalem, these words were mentioned:
"They will be his people, and God Himself will be with them
and be their God."

With regards to the New and Everlasting Covenant, the Lord
mentioned these words: "I will be their God, and they will be
my people."

Therefore, the coming of the New Jerusalem is the fulfillment
of the New and Everlasting Covenant.

CHAPTER 12

COMPLETE UNITY IN THE LAST DAYS

May they be one as We are one.
(John 17:22 NIV)

Are we prepared for the Last Days?

We are now in the Last Days! This is a dreadful thing to hear if we do not know what it means. But if we do understand it fully well, this is the moment we have been waiting for. Many generations of believers have waited for this in full eagerness.

They all believed that their generation was the last—from the generation of Christians during the New Testament era down to the generation that preceded us.

We are now in the Last Days! Our generation must believe this without any shadow of doubt. We need not ask if we are now into it because, indeed, we are now in the Last Days.

Are we really prepared?

The Lord Jesus said:

> Therefore keep watch, because you do not know on what day your Lord will come … So you also must be ready, because the Son of Man will come at an hour when you do not expect him. (Matthew 24:42–44 NIV)

First, the Lord Jesus said we do not know the day. Second, He will come at an hour when we do not expect Him. His conclusion: we must keep watch, and we must be ready.

Therefore, the Lord's Second Coming is a matter of being prepared. But how do we prepare?

The Apostle Paul wrote:

> Now, brothers, about times and dates we do not need to write to you, for you know very well that the day of the Lord will come like a thief in the night … But you, brothers, are not in darkness so that this day should surprise you like a thief. You are all sons of the light and sons of the day. We do not belong to the night or to the darkness. (1 Thessalonians 5:1–5 NIV)

First, the Apostle Paul said that there is no need for him to write about times and dates. Second, he confirmed that the day of the Lord will come like a thief in the night. Third, he stressed that the day of the Lord will not be a surprise for those who are sons of the light. Since we belong to the light, the Lord's Second Coming will not surprise us. We may not know the exact date and the exact time, but somehow we will know.

The Lord Jesus said:

> That servant who knows his master's will and does not
> get ready or does not do what his master wants will be
> beaten with many blows. (Luke 12:47 NIV)

Therefore, the Lord's Second Coming is a matter of knowing
what our Master wants so that we can prepare. What then does
our Master want?

What will happen in the Last Days shall be in accordance with
what our Master wants. If we know what our Master wants,
then we will know how to prepare. The best way to prepare is
to do actions that are in agreement with what will happen in
the Last Days.

The Apostle Paul wrote:

> This is good, and pleases God our Savior, *who wants all
> men to be saved* and *to come to a knowledge of the truth.*
> (1 Timothy 2:3–4 NIV, emphasis added)

> I am not ashamed of the gospel, because it is *the power
> of God for the salvation* of everyone who believes: first
> for the Jew, then for the Gentile. (Romans 1:16 NIV,
> emphasis added)

The Apostle Peter wrote:

> You ought to live holy and godly lives *as you look
> forward to the day of God and speed its coming.* (2 Peter
> 3:10–11 NIV, emphasis added)

What our Master wants is the salvation of all men. This means that in the Last Days, the gospel will be preached at its most increased measure so that many will be saved. Also, living holy and godly lives (living according to the gospel—right testimony) can speed up the Lord's coming.

Therefore, the Lord's Second Coming is a matter of accomplishing our Master's will—the preaching of the gospel as a testimony.

The Lord Jesus said:

> And this gospel of the kingdom will be preached in the whole world as a *testimony* to all nations, and then the end will come. (Matthew 24:14 NIV, emphasis added)

The preaching of the gospel as a testimony indicates that the gospel must be backed up by evidence. The gospel means good news; that is, good things will first happen to those who will proclaim it. And then good things will result to those who will hear and believe it. To be in the right testimony means to be in the right position.

Therefore, in these Last Days, in order for the gospel to be preached as a testimony in the whole world, God will place His people in the right position spiritually—this is the church in complete unity.

In these Last Days, do not be surprised if you hear, everywhere, many messages about unity. For God will raise up many preachers from all around the globe—all will be preaching about unity. The reason is obvious—testimony.

The Bible declared:

> Hear, O Israel: The LORD our God, the LORD is
> one. (Deuteronomy 6:4 NIV)

Our God is one. To be in the right position spiritually means
there must be unity for all the believers. We cannot preach the
gospel as a testimony if we proclaim that our God is one yet
we are not one in heart and in action.

Unity means we are many yet we are one. We were created after
God's own image, after His own likeness. There is the Father,
there is Jesus, and there is the Holy Spirit—three distinct
persons yet together as one—the perfect picture of the perfect
unity.

By complete unity in the Last Days, God will place His people
in the right position spiritually. This was promised by God,
prayed for by the Lord Jesus, and powered by the Holy Spirit.

By now we may be wondering if complete unity is really possible
among the believers. With the efforts of man, this is really
impossible, but not with God. We have denominational, racial,
cultural, social, educational, emotional, and other differences.
Given all these, churches and believers are impossible to unite.

But God, not man, will do it in the Last Days. Let us again
enumerate at least three reasons why complete unity will
certainly happen in the Last Days:

(1) Complete unity was promised by God.
(2) Complete unity was prayed for by the Lord Jesus.
(3) Complete unity will be powered by the Holy Spirit.

Promised By God

Under the New Covenant, God declared:

> They will be my people, and I will be their God. I
> will give them *singleness of heart and action*. (Jeremiah
> 32:38–39 NIV, emphasis added)

To be called God's people means whoever God is, we will
be. God is holy; we will also be holy. God is one; we will also
become one. God promises that we will be in complete unity
(He will give us singleness of heart and action) so that we
will fear Him, and this is for our own good. This means that
complete unity in the church will cause God's goodness and
blessings to flow unto us, and this will also cause us to do good
since we are God's people.

Also, being holy and godly, as the Apostle Peter declared, will
speed up the Second Coming of our Lord Jesus.

Prayed for by the Lord Jesus

The Lord Jesus prayed:

> Holy Father, protect them by the power of your
> name—the name you gave me—so that *they may be
> one as we are one*. (John 17:11 NIV, emphasis added)

For the disciples to become one, the Lord Jesus prayed that
they be protected from the evil one. The devil is not threatened
as long as we are not united—no testimony! He knows that if
the church is not united, the preaching of the gospel will be of
no effect, as described by the following passage:

> May they be *brought to complete unity to let the world*
> *know that you sent me* and have loved them even as you
> have loved me. (John 17:23 NIV, emphasis added)

Without complete unity, the world will not know that Jesus
was sent by the Father. The preaching of the gospel and
complete unity must go together—with testimony!

Powered by the Holy Spirit

God declared:

> See, I will send you the prophet Elijah before that great
> and dreadful day of the LORD comes. He will turn the
> hearts of the fathers to their children, and the hearts
> of the children to their fathers; or else I will come and
> strike the land with a curse. (Malachi 4:5–6 NIV)

Before the first coming of the Lord Jesus, John the Baptist was
referred to as:

> And he will go on before the Lord, *in the spirit and*
> *power of Elijah*, to turn the hearts of the parents to
> their children and the disobedient to the wisdom of
> the righteous—to make ready a people prepared for
> the Lord. (Luke 1:17 NIV, emphasis added)

Elijah did come, not as himself but as a man (John the Baptist)
empowered by the Holy Spirit. In these Last Days, before the
Second Coming of the Lord Jesus, God will use people who
will go on before the Lord—in the spirit and power of Elijah
(to turn the hearts of the fathers to their children and the
hearts of the children to their fathers). This is to uphold unity
within the church as powered by the Holy Spirit.

There is power in unity! The heavens and the earth, seen and unseen things, were created by the united efforts of the Father, the Lord Jesus, and the Holy Spirit.

The tower of Babel story narrates how man's plan can be made achievable (nothing can be impossible) through unity:

> But the LORD came down to see the city and the tower that the men were building. The LORD said, "If as one people speaking the same language they have begun to do this, then *nothing they plan to do will be impossible* for them. Come, let us go down and confuse their language so they will not understand each other." (Genesis 11:5–7 NIV, emphasis added)

Our God acknowledged that nothing would be impossible for these ungodly if they united as one people. In these Last Days, if the godly will unite as one in doing the will of God, how much greater exploits do you think will they accomplish?

King David, the man after God's own heart, wrote:

> How good and pleasant it is when brothers live together in unity! It is like precious *oil* poured on the head, running down on the beard, running down on Aaron's beard, down upon the collar of his robes. It is as if the *dew* of Hermon were falling on Mount Zion. *For there the LORD bestows his blessing*, even life forevermore. (Psalms 133 NIV, emphasis added)

Unity among brothers is compared to two things: the oil and the dew. The oil speaks of the anointing—the Holy Spirit working powerfully through godly people. The dew falling on the soil will make the soil fertile—it speaks of prosperity.

Where there is unity, there the Lord bestows His blessing—the blessing of anointing and the blessing of prosperity. Without unity there is no blessing. Because of complete unity, God's promises of blessing will be bestowed, and the preaching of the gospel as a testimony will be fulfilled. Therefore, complete unity will prepare the Second Coming of our King.

What is complete unity?

The first generations of believers, as mentioned in the book of Acts, were known for their great accomplishments, as they were filled and empowered by the Holy Spirit. They preached the gospel accompanied by working of healings, miracles, signs, and great wonders. They were able to do these great undertakings because they were united in heart and action, as narrated by the following passage:

> They devoted themselves to the apostles' teaching and to fellowship, to the breaking of bread and to prayer … All the believers were together and had everything in common. They sold property and possessions to give to anyone who had need. Every day they continued to meet together in the temple courts. They broke bread in their homes and ate together with glad and sincere hearts, praising God and enjoying the favor of all the people. And the Lord added to their number daily those who were being saved. (Acts 2:42–47 NIV)

Seven in the Bible describes completeness, so let us enumerate from the above passage seven things to make unity complete:

(1) Unity in teaching—the New Covenant teaching
(2) Unity in fellowship
(3) Unity in purpose and vision

(4) Unity in prayer
(5) Unity on finances
(6) Unity in praise and worship
(7) Unity in preaching the pure gospel

The church during the early times (as described in the book of Acts) had set an example for us to follow. If they were able to accomplish great things during their stay inside of time, the last generation of believers before the Second Coming is expected to do greater. In order for this to happen there will be complete unity in the church.

> "This is the covenant I will make with the house of Israel after that time," declares the LORD. "I will put my law in their minds and write it on their hearts. I will be their God, and they will be my people." (Jeremiah 31:33–34; Hebrews 8:10–12 NIV)

The phrase "I will be their God, and they will be my people" speaks of the following:

> They will be my people, and I will be their God. I will give them *singleness of heart and action* ... I will make an *everlasting covenant* with them: *I will never stop doing good to them ... I will rejoice in doing them good ... I will give them all the prosperity I have promised them*. (Jeremiah 32:38–42 NIV, emphasis added)

The only term is to be one in heart and action—the benefit: awesome blessings!

The Apostle Paul wrote:

> "For this reason a man will leave his father and mother and be united to his wife, and the two will become one flesh." This is a profound mystery—but I am talking about Christ and the church. (Ephesians 5:29–32 NIV)

The phrase "and the two will become one flesh" speaks of two things:

(1) A man and a woman joined together in marriage
(2) The Lord Jesus Christ and the church also joined together in marriage

In both cases, there is unity on finances. All our properties belong to Jesus, and all the properties of Jesus belong to us—good news! Complete unity always includes unity on finances.

Let us read the following passage:

> All the believers were one in heart and mind. No one claimed that any of his possessions was his own, but they shared everything they had. With great power the apostles continued to testify to the resurrection of the Lord Jesus, and much grace was upon them all. There were no needy persons among them. (Acts 4:32–35 NIV)

This is a manifestation of Psalm 133. Where there is complete unity, God bestows anointing and prosperity:

(1) All the believers were one in heart and mind, and they shared everything they had—this is complete unity.

(2) With great power the apostles continued to testify—this is anointing.

(3) Much grace was upon them all, and there were no needy persons among them—this is prosperity.

With regards to the prosperity of the church in the Last Days, this was prophesied and will surely happen for the sake of the gospel and with relation to complete unity. This prophecy was foretold with reference to the New Covenant tithing.

Levites in the Old Covenant:

> I have taken the Levites from among the Israelites in place of the first male offspring of every Israelite woman. The Levites are mine, for all the firstborn are mine. (Numbers 3:12–13 NIV)

Levites in the New Covenant:

> But you are a chosen people, a royal priesthood, a holy nation, a people belonging to God. (1 Peter 2:9 NIV)

Scripture states that perfection could not be attained through the Levitical priesthood (the reason why there is still need for another priest to come)—one in the order of Melchizedek (this is the Lord Jesus), not in the order of Aaron. There is a change of the priesthood; therefore, there must also be a change of the Law.

In the Old Covenant, the Old Covenant Levites were the ones receiving the tithes. In the New Covenant, the New Covenant Levites (the church) will be the ones to receive the tithes.

Tithing in the Old Covenant:

> Will a man rob God? Yet you rob me. But you ask, "How do we rob you? In tithes and offerings. You are under a curse—the whole nation of you—because you are robbing me ... Test me in this," says the Lord Almighty, "and see if I will not throw open the floodgates of heaven and pour out so much blessing ... I will prevent pests from devouring your crops." (Malachi 3:8–11 NIV)

In the Old Covenant, those who are giving their tithes will be blessed, and those who are not giving their tithes will be cursed.

Tithing in the New Covenant:

> One might even say that Levi, who collects the tenth, paid the tenth through Abraham, because when Melchizedek met Abraham, Levi was still in the body of his ancestor. (Hebrews 7:9–10 NIV)

> Then Abram gave him a tenth of everything. (Genesis 14:20 NIV)

> And Abraham said to God, "If only *Ishmael* might live under your blessing!" Then God said, "Yes ... I have heard you: I will *surely bless* him; I will make him *fruitful* and will greatly increase his numbers. He will be the *father of twelve rulers*, and I will make him into a *great nation*. But my covenant I will establish with Isaac." (Genesis 17:18–21 NIV, emphasis added)

From the above passages, it is clearly mentioned that even Levi (who collected tithes) also gave tithes through Abraham to Melchizedek (representing the Lord Jesus). It was Abraham who gave tithes to Melchizedek, and technically it follows that all his descendants also gave tithes—and that includes both Israel and Ishmael. Ishmael was also blessed by God because that was His promise to Abraham.

All were required to give tithes to God because all tithes belong to God. But God assigned the Levites to receive tithes because that was their portion (God does not really need the tithes, but this He established for the sake of the Levites).

In the New Covenant, God called his people as a royal priesthood—a Levitical priesthood not in the order of Aaron but in the order of Melchizedek (the Lord Jesus, our High Priest). And in the Last Days, God will command all people and all races (those who belong to the Old Covenant) to give their tithes to the New Covenant Levites—and God will surely curse anyone who will not follow this command. Just as in the day of the Exodus of the Israelites from the land of Egypt, New Covenant people will plunder the wealth of the wicked as they enter the New Jerusalem—for the sake of the gospel (right position not only spiritually but also financially).

This is actually the prophecy of prosperity as promised by God to his chosen people (those who belong to the New Covenant), as described by the following passages:

> And you will again see the distinction between the righteous and the wicked, between those who serve God and those who do not. (Malachi 3:18 NIV)

> They will be my people, and I will be their God. I will give them *singleness* of *heart* and *action* ... I will

give them all the *prosperity* I have promised them. (Jeremiah 32:38–42 NIV, emphasis added)

This prosperity will happen in the Last Days because there will be complete unity in the church (right testimony).

As mentioned in chapter 1 of this book, the church will face a difficult stage before the Second Coming of the Lord Jesus. This pertains to the mixture of the New Covenant teaching with the Old Covenant teaching or human traditions. We have called this mixture the Babylon conflict—discussed in almost all the chapters of this book. The only instruction the Lord Jesus has given us before His Second Coming is to come out of this mixture of teachings.

Therefore, for the church to be in complete unity in the Last Days, there must be only one teaching—we must devote ourselves to the apostles' teaching, which refers to the New and Everlasting Covenant teaching.

Apostles and Prophets in the Last Days

During the early stage of the church, apostles and prophets were used to build up and keep the church united, as narrated by the following passages:

> Consequently, you are no longer foreigners and strangers, but fellow citizens with God's people and also members of his household, *built on the foundation of the apostles and prophets*, with Christ Jesus himself as the chief cornerstone. (Ephesians 2:11–22 NIV, emphasis added)

> So Christ himself gave the *apostles*, the *prophets*, the *evangelists*, the *pastors* and *teachers*, to equip his people

for works of service, so that the body of Christ may be built up *until we all reach unity* in the faith and in the knowledge of the Son of God. (Ephesians 4:11–13 NIV, emphasis added)

The Lord Jesus has equipped the church to be united by using and anointing five ministry people: (1) apostles, (2) prophets, (3) evangelists, (4) pastors, and (5) teachers.

And He even mentioned that apostles and prophets were the foundation of unity, with Himself as the chief cornerstone. Nowadays, notice that the apostles and prophets (foundation of unity) were not even mentioned within the local churches. We have evangelists, pastors, and teachers. But where are the apostles and the prophets?

Let us read the following passages:

Rejoice over her, you heavens! Rejoice, you people of God! Rejoice, *apostles and prophets*! For God has judged her with the judgment she imposed on you ... With such violence the great city of *Babylon* will be thrown down, never to be found again. (Revelation 18:20–21 NIV, emphasis added)

And showed me the *Holy City, Jerusalem*, coming down out of heaven from God ... *The wall of the city had twelve foundations*, and on them were the names of the twelve *apostles* of the Lamb. (Revelation 21:9–14 NIV, emphasis added)

In these Last Days, God will restore the foundation of unity (the ministry of the apostles and of the prophets) in order to place His people in the right position by enforcing one, and only one, teaching—the New Covenant teaching.

To emphasize, before the Second Coming of the Lord Jesus, God will place His people in the right position spiritually—this is the church in complete unity.

CONCLUDING LESSONS

NEW COVENANT REPRESENTATIONS

And this gospel of the kingdom will be preached in
the whole world as a testimony to all nations, and
then the end will come. (Matthew 24:14 NIV)

As mentioned in the introduction of this book, if we truly
want to know that the Second Coming is really very near, all
we need to do is look at the current condition of the church.
Also, the very reason the Lord Jesus will come back is for
the bride—a ready church that is united, without spot, and
without blemish.

What is keeping the church from being one has something
to do with Laodicea—the church is still neither hot nor
cold. As discussed all through this book, there is a mixture
of New Covenant teaching and Old Covenant teaching,
which is what keeps the church from being united. This
is the Babylon conflict, which is the final conflict in the
church.

To conclude, there are three pillars that will make complete unity in the church to come about in the Last Days. These three pillars are the following:

(1) The Holy Spirit
(2) Fellowship
(3) The gospel of the kingdom (New Covenant teaching)

The first two were already given, but the third one is yet to be seen and accomplished in the church. As prophesied, the church needed to complete the seven major stages of the one journey that was set before the beginning of time. But at the end of this journey (which is in the Last Days), the Holy Spirit will uphold unity to the highest degree in the fellowship of the believers by giving them one, and only one, pure teaching—the New and Everlasting Covenant teaching (the gospel of the kingdom)—without mixture and contamination by the Old Covenant teaching and human traditions.

We'll discuss some scripture passages that give emphasis and representation to the New and Everlasting Covenant. These will guide and help us to realize and distinguish between New Covenant teaching and Old Covenant teaching or human traditions. After completely reading this book, you will be able to teach passages from the Bible by receiving revelations from the Holy Spirit and discovering truths about the New and Everlasting Covenant, which is the eternal gospel.

Go through the concluding lessons, and add the revelations that you will receive at the end of each lesson so that you will be able to teach others about this wonderful message in preparing the church for the Second Coming of our King.

The Story of Job and His Friends

> In the land of Uz there lived a man whose name was
> Job. This man was blameless and upright; he feared
> God and shunned evil ... He was the greatest man
> among all the people of the East. (Job 1:1–3 NIV)

This story is normally relayed by highlighting the life of Job,
who was described as righteous, very wealthy, and having a
wonderful family. But following the events that took place
in the presence of the Lord involving angels and Satan, there
came, suddenly, a series of catastrophic events that put Job to
the test. At the end of these tough times, Job stood victorious
and remained faithful to his God. Then his latter days were
described as more blessed than his former days had been.

It is sad to say that this kind of portrayal tends to hide the truth
behind the story. This is not a New Covenant representation but
rather an Old Covenant or human-traditions representation.
The real story unfolds when three close friends visited Job
to comfort him during his great suffering. One important
question rambled in Job's mind, and he needed to search
quickly to find a satisfying answer.

"Why would a covenant-keeping God be willing to break His
covenant?" Job could not accept the fact that he was actually
suffering in spite of his great effort to remain blameless and
upright in the eyes of his God by upholding the covenant. Let
us read some of the passages from the book of Job to take hold
of the real story:

> When Job's three friends, Eliphaz the Temanite, Bildad
> the Shuhite and Zophar the Naamathite, heard about all
> the troubles that had come upon him, they set out from

their homes and met together by agreement to go and
sympathize with him and comfort him … Then they sat
on the ground with him *for seven days and seven nights.
No one said a word to him*, because they saw *how great
his suffering* was. (Job 2:11–13 NIV, emphasis added)

After seven days and seven nights of saying nothing, Job broke
the silence, but his words made his friends wonder. They all
alternately argued with him (instead of comforting him),
which resulted in heated discussion.

The book of Job has a total of forty-two chapters, but this is
the summary of their heartfelt conversation:

Job—"Let the day of my birth be erased, and the night I was
conceived. Let that day be turned to darkness. Let it be
lost even to God on high, and let no light shine on it …
Why didn't I die as I came from the womb?"

Eliphaz—"In the past you have encouraged many people;
you have strengthened those who were weak … But
now when trouble strikes, you lose heart. You are
terrified when it touches you … Stop and think! Do the
innocent die? When have the upright been destroyed?
My experience shows that those who plant trouble and
cultivate evil will harvest the same."

Job—"Stop assuming my guilt, for I have done no wrong.
Do you think I am lying? Don't I know the difference
between right and wrong? … If I have sinned, what have
I done to you, O watcher of all humanity? Why make
me your target? Am I a burden to you?"

Bildad—"How long will you go on like this? You sound like a blustering wind. Does God twist justice? Does the Almighty twist what is right? Your children must have sinned against him, so their punishment was well deserved. But if you pray to God and seek the favor of the Almighty, and if you are pure and live with integrity, he will surely rise up and restore your happy home."

Job—"But how can a person be declared innocent in God's sight? If someone wanted to take God to court, would it be possible to answer him even once in a thousand times? ... Even if I were right, I would have no defense. I could only plead for mercy. And even if I summoned him and he responded, I'm not sure he would listen to me."

Zophar—"Shouldn't someone answer this torrent of words? ... You claim, 'My beliefs are pure,' and 'I am clean in the sight of God.' If only God would speak; if only he would tell you what he thinks! ... Get rid of your sins, and leave all iniquity behind you. Then your face will brighten with innocence. You will be strong and free of fear."

Job—"You are no better than I am. As for me, I would speak directly to the Almighty. I want to argue my case with God himself. As for you, you smear me with lies. As physicians, you are worthless quacks. If only you could be silent! That's the wisest thing you could do ... Be silent now and leave me alone. Let me speak, and I will face the consequences ... O God, tell me, what have I done wrong? Show me my rebellion and my sin. Why do you turn away from me? Why do you treat me as your enemy?"

Eliphaz—"What do you know that we don't? What do you understand that we do not? ... If you will listen, I will show you. I will answer you from my own experience ... The wicked writhe in pain throughout their lives. Years of trouble are stored up for the ruthless?"

Job—"I have heard all this before. What miserable comforters you are! ... God hates me and angrily tears me apart. He snaps his teeth at me and pierces me with his eyes. People jeer and laugh at me. They slap my cheek in contempt. A mob gathers against me."

Bildad—"How long before you stop talking? Speak sense if you want us to answer! Do you think we are mere animals? Do you think we are stupid? ... They will say, 'This was the home of a wicked person, the place of one who rejected God.'"

Job—"How long will you torture me? How long will you try to crush me with your words? You have already insulted me ten times ... You think you're better than I am, using my humiliation as evidence of my sin. But it is God who has wronged me, capturing me in his net ... Have mercy on me, my friends, have mercy, for the hand of God has struck me. Must you also persecute me, like God does? Haven't you chewed me up enough?"

Zophar—"I must reply because I am greatly disturbed. I've had to endure your insults, but now my spirit prompts me to reply. Don't you realize that from the beginning of time, ever since people were first placed on the earth, the triumph of the wicked has been short lived and the joy of the godless has been only temporary?"

Job—"Listen closely to what I am saying. That's one consolation you can give me. Bear with me, and let me speak. After I have spoken, you may resume mocking me ... Why do the wicked prosper, growing old and powerful? Their homes are safe from every fear, and God does not punish them ... They spend their days in prosperity, then go down to the grave in peace. And yet they say to God, 'Go away. We want no part of you and your ways' ... So how can you console me with your nonsense? Nothing is left of your answers but falsehood!"

And so those tough and heartbreaking words continued until God intervened.

Job's friends believed that the righteous would surely be blessed, while the wicked would definitely be cursed—that was the covenant they knew God had established for mankind. They believed that God would never break His covenant, so it follows that they considered Job somehow had broken the covenant, which was the cause of his trouble and suffering. Job believed otherwise. He knew, with his whole heart, that he was blameless and righteous and had never broken the covenant; thus, he concluded that God had broken the covenant.

At the end of the story, God spoke with Job and made him comprehend why He had allowed him to undergo all those aches and great sufferings. He showed Job the answer to the question: "Why would a covenant-keeping God be willing to break His covenant?"

God introduced to Job the one true covenant (the new and everlasting covenant, which was based on God's grace and mercy) and showed that the former covenant (the Old Covenant, which was based on man's effort) was already obsolete and was not really made for the righteous. The book of Job concluded as follows:

> "You have not spoken the truth about me, as my servant Job has." So Eliphaz the Temanite, Bildad the Shuhite and Zophar the Naamathite did what the LORD told them; and the LORD accepted Job's prayer. After Job had prayed for his friends, the LORD restored his fortunes and gave him twice as much as he had before ... *The LORD blessed the latter part of Job's life more than the former part.* (Job 42:7–12 NIV, emphasis added)

Indeed, the glory of the New Covenant surpasses the glory of the Old Covenant.

Write your revelations here: _____
_____
_____
_____
_____
_____
_____
_____
_____
_____
_____
_____
_____
_____
_____
_____
_____
_____

Cain and Abel

> By faith Abel brought God a better offering than Cain did. By faith he was commended as righteous, when God spoke well of his offerings. And by faith Abel still speaks, even though he is dead. (Hebrews 11:4 NIV)

Cain represents the Old Covenant people (those who failed to bring acceptable offerings to God—by works), while Abel represents the New Covenant people (those commended as righteous by God because of their offerings—by faith).

Write your revelations here: _____

_____

_____

_____

_____

_____

_____

_____

_____

_____

_____

_____

_____

_____

_____

_____

_____

_____

_____

_____

_____

Ishmael and Isaac

> The women represent two covenants. One covenant is from Mount Sinai and bears children who are to be slaves: This is Hagar. Now Hagar stands for Mount Sinai in Arabia and corresponds to the present city of Jerusalem, because she is in slavery with her children. But the Jerusalem that is above is free, and she is our mother. (Galatians 4:21–31 NIV)

Hagar represents the Old Covenant, and her son, Ishmael, represents Old Covenant people (those born according to the flesh and who are to be slaves). Sarah represents the New Covenant, and her son, Isaac, represents New Covenant people (those born as the result of a divine promise, those born by the power of the Spirit, and those who are to be free).

Write your revelations here: _____

_____

_____

_____

_____

_____

_____

_____

_____

_____

_____

_____

_____

_____

_____

_____

_____

_____

Esau and Jacob

> Yet, before the twins were born or had done anything
> good or bad—in order that God's purpose in election
> might stand: not by works but by him who calls—she
> was told, "The older will serve the younger." Just as it
> is written: "Jacob I loved, but Esau I hated." (Romans
> 9:10–13 NIV)

Esau represents the Old Covenant people (those hated by God
and those who failed to receive the blessing of the firstborn),
while Jacob represents the New Covenant people (those loved
by God and chosen by God to receive the blessing of the
firstborn).

Write your revelations here: _____

_____

_____

_____

_____

_____

_____

_____

_____

_____

_____

_____

_____

_____

_____

_____

_____

_____

Manasseh and Ephraim

> And Joseph took both of them, Ephraim on his right toward Israel's left hand and Manasseh on his left toward Israel's right hand, and brought them close to him. But Israel reached out his right hand and put it on Ephraim's head, though he was the younger, and crossing his arms, he put his left hand on Manasseh's head, even though Manasseh was the firstborn. (Genesis 48:13–14 NIV)

Manasseh represents the Old Covenant people (those who failed to receive the blessing of the firstborn), while Ephraim represents the New Covenant people (those chosen by God to receive the blessing of the firstborn).

Write your revelations here: _____

_____

_____

_____

_____

_____

_____

_____

_____

_____

_____

_____

_____

_____

_____

_____

_____

The Prodigal Son and His Brother

> The older brother became angry and refused to go in. So his father went out and pleaded with him. But he answered his father, "Look! All these years I've been slaving for you and never disobeyed your orders. Yet you never gave me even a young goat so I could celebrate with my friends. But when this son of yours who has squandered your property with prostitutes comes home, you kill the fattened calf for him!" (Luke 15:11–32 NIV)

The man in the story was described as a loving father with two sons, great wealth, and many servants. Everything was going well, and all enjoyed prosperity under his care. But one day the younger son decided to come out of his father's care and demanded that his share of his rightful inheritance be given to him. The father consented, so the son went on his way to live a merry life, spending everything he had until nothing was left. The son became very poor and had to toil as a hired worker tending pigs. He was so poor that he even ate food intended for the pigs.

Then he realized how foolish he was, so he planned to go back to his father, no longer as a son but as one of his father's hired servants. When that time came for him to see his father, he saw a completely different atmosphere than what he was expecting.

The father prepared a great celebration to welcome him, not as a hired servant but as his long-lost, beloved son. The other son was disappointed with the action of his father.

The older son represents Old Covenant people (those who work according to the flesh). The younger son represents New

Covenant people (those who were accepted and forgiven as a result of God's mercy and compassion).

Write your revelations here: _____

_____

_____

_____

_____

_____

_____

_____

_____

_____

_____

_____

_____

_____

_____

_____

_____

_____

_____

_____

_____

_____

_____

_____

_____

_____

_____

_____

_____

The Vineyard Workers

> For the kingdom of heaven is like a landowner who went out early in the morning to hire workers for his vineyard. (Matthew 20:1–16 NIV)

The Lord Jesus compared the kingdom of heaven to a landowner who hired workers for one day for his vineyard. Each batch of workers differed in length of working time so that those who had worked longer expected to receive more. But at the end of the day, when the work was finished, each received the same amount of wages not considering how much time they had worked. When confronted, the landowner answered: "Friend, I haven't been unfair! Didn't you agree to work all day for the usual wage? Take your money and go. I wanted to pay this last worker the same as you. Is it against the law for me to do what I want with my money? Should you be jealous because I am kind to others?"

The vineyard workers who were hired first represent Old Covenant people (those who receive wages according to their works). The vineyard workers who were hired last represent New Covenant people (those who receive blessings according to God's generosity).

Write your revelations here: _____

_____
_____
_____
_____
_____
_____
_____
_____

The Withered Fig Tree

> Early in the morning, as Jesus was on his way back to the city, he was hungry. Seeing a fig tree by the road, he went up to it but found nothing on it except leaves. Then he said to it, "May you never bear fruit again!" Immediately the tree withered. (Matthew 21:18–20 NIV)

Why would Jesus curse a fig tree just because it had no fruit? To understand this we need to connect it to the story of Adam and Eve after they ate from the forbidden tree, as narrated in the book of Genesis: "At that moment their eyes were opened, and they suddenly felt shame at their nakedness. So they sewed fig leaves together to cover themselves."

The use of fig leaves as covering represents man's first effort after falling to the Old Covenant (eating the fruit from the tree of the knowledge of good and evil). The withered fig tree represents the release of God's people from the Law so that they can serve in the new way of the Spirit (the Lord Jesus had the fig tree withered to show New Covenant people that they were free from the Old Covenant).

Write your revelations here: _____
_____
_____
_____
_____
_____
_____
_____
_____
_____

Ananias and Sapphira

> Now a man named Ananias, together with his wife
> Sapphira, also sold a piece of property. With his wife's
> full knowledge he kept back part of the money for
> himself, but brought the rest and put it at the apostles'
> feet. (Acts 5:1–11 NIV)

Why would God judge Ananias and Sapphira just because they
lied about money? To understand this we need to know the
meaning of the names of the couple: the name *Ananias* means
"grace" (New Covenant), and the name *Sapphira* means "law"
(Old Covenant). Their union represents the combining of the
New Covenant and the Old Covenant (which is Babylon).
Their judgment represents the destruction of Babylon (God
is showing His people that the gospel must be pure and not
contaminated). When Jesus said that we couldn't serve two
masters, He was also implying that we couldn't mix two
covenants.

Write your revelations here:_____
_____
_____
_____
_____
_____
_____
_____
_____
_____
_____
_____
_____
_____

The Two Systems

> The master commended the dishonest manager because he had acted shrewdly. For the people of this world are more shrewd in dealing with their own kind than are the people of the light. (Luke 16:8 NIV)

Why would God commend the dishonest manager for acting shrewdly? Scripture mentions two kinds of people: the people of this world (those who belong to the Old Covenant) and the people of the light (those who belong to the New and Everlasting Covenant). The Lord Jesus is saying that the people of this world act according to their natural system (according to the flesh), but the people of the light do not act according to their natural system (according to the Spirit). He commended the dishonest manager to convey this message.

Write your revelations here: _____

_____

_____

_____

_____

_____

_____

_____

_____

_____

_____

_____

_____

_____

_____

_____

A Man Reaps What He Sows

> Do not be deceived: God cannot be mocked. A man reaps what he sows. Whoever sows to please their flesh, from the flesh will reap destruction; whoever sows to please the Spirit, from the Spirit will reap eternal life. (Galatians 6:7–8 NIV)

Those who sow to please their flesh (sowing in accordance with the Old Covenant) will reap destruction; those who sow to please the Spirit (sowing in accordance with the New and Everlasting Covenant) will reap eternal life.

Write your revelations here: _____

_____
_____
_____
_____
_____
_____
_____
_____
_____
_____
_____
_____
_____
_____
_____
_____
_____
_____
_____
_____

Who Overcomes?

> For everyone born of God overcomes the world. This is the victory that has overcome the world, even our faith. Who is it that overcomes the world? Only the one who believes that Jesus is the Son of God. (1 John 5:1–5 NIV)

The Old Covenant people are not born of God (without faith and cannot overcome the world). The New Covenant people are born of God (with faith in the Lord Jesus and have overcome the world).

Write your revelations here: _____

_____

_____

_____

_____

_____

_____

_____

_____

_____

_____

_____

_____

_____

_____

_____

_____

_____

_____

_____

The New Covenant Commandments

> And this is his command: *to believe* in the name of his Son, Jesus Christ, and *to love* one another as he commanded us. The one who keeps God's commands lives in him, and he in them. *And this is how we know that he lives in us: We know it by the Spirit he gave us.* (1 John 3:23–24 NIV, emphasis added)

Love for God means to keep his commands. These commands are not the rules and regulations from the Law (Old Covenant), which are followed using human effort. Everyone who thinks that God's commands are from the Law is bound to failure.

The only one bound to victory is the one who follows the true commandments (to believe in the Lord Jesus and to love one another)—the New Covenant commandments.

Write your revelations here: _____

_____

_____

_____

_____

_____

_____

_____

_____

_____

_____

_____

_____

_____

_____

The Required Weight

> *Tekel*: You have been weighed on the scales and found
> wanting. (Daniel 5:27 NIV)

The Old Covenant people have been weighed on the scales
and found wanting. The New Covenant people have achieved
the required weight because of their faith in the Lord Jesus.

In terms of number, seven has always been God's perfect
requirement—it speaks of completeness. Numbers one to six
speak of work—the work of creation was done for six days.
The seventh day was declared by God as a Sabbath rest for His
people—all that was required was already completed.

To be precise, number six is the number of man; for on the
sixth day, man was created. It speaks of human effort, which
is the requirement in the Old Covenant but not in the New
Covenant. Man's effort (number six) can never achieve God's
required weight (number seven); only by resting and believing
in the Lord Jesus can God's required weight be achieved.

In the first conflict (Canaan conflict), from eternity, man has
rejected the Eternal Covenant (being one with God) and has
chosen another covenant (being independent of God and being
dependent on man's effort). Man was weighed on the scales
and found wanting—the first number six.

In the second conflict (Egypt conflict), inside of time, man
has combined Old Covenant teaching with human traditions.
Man was weighed on the scales and found wanting—the
second number six.

In the third and final conflict (Babylon conflict), before the ending of time, man has contaminated the New Covenant teaching with Old Covenant teaching and human traditions. Man was weighed on the scales and found wanting—the third number six.

These seem to be the reasons why the book of Revelation mentions that all whose names have not been written in the Lamb's book of life were forced to receive the mark of the beast—666. Old Covenant people always rely on man's effort.

Write your revelations here: _____

_____
_____
_____
_____
_____
_____
_____
_____
_____
_____
_____
_____
_____
_____
_____
_____
_____
_____
_____
_____
_____
_____

REMARKS FROM
THE AUTHOR

My dear reader, I want to thank you for taking time to read this book. The fact that it is now in your hands means that God divinely appointed this. It is not an accident. May you find this useful in seeking to know more about the Lord Jesus and His Second Coming, and may it be a good source of information to prepare you for that great and most awaited event in these Last Days.

But just like all other books that may be considered somewhat fictional or more likely opinionated, this book is not exempt from having mistake or error. How then do you know the truth?

Let me share with you the Bible's golden rule in seeking answers to any questions. The scripture states:

> We know it by the Spirit he gave us. (1 John 3:24 NIV)

> But the Advocate, the Holy Spirit, whom the Father will send in my name, will teach you all things and will remind you of everything I have said to you. (John 14:26 NIV)

> As for you, the anointing you received from him remains in you, and you do not need anyone to teach

you. But as his anointing teaches you about all things and as that anointing is real, not counterfeit—just as it has taught you, remain in him. (1 John 2:27 NIV)

The man without the Spirit does not accept the things that come from the Spirit of God, for they are foolishness to him, and he cannot understand them, because they are spiritually discerned. (1 Corinthians 2:14 NIV)

The golden rule while we are still inside of time is the Holy Spirit is our Guide, our Teacher, our Friend, our Counselor, and the Life and Power of the church.

While inside of time, God's chosen people (whose names have been written in the Lamb's Book of Life) are all connected to the Father and the Lord Jesus because of the Holy Spirit.

If you find this book personally beneficial, share it with your friends. Give it as a gift to your loved ones. In doing so, you are taking part in preparing the church for the Second Coming of our King.

The Lord Jesus says, "Yes, I am coming soon."

Amen. Come, Lord Jesus.

The grace of the Lord Jesus be with God's people. Amen.

To the beloved people of God, whose names have been written in the Book of Life from the creation of the world before the beginning of time, catch the vision and be a part of the mission.

Vision:
To see God's chosen people come out of
Babylon and enter the New Jerusalem

Mission:
In order for God's chosen people
to be prepared for the Second Coming of the Lord Jesus,
there must be complete unity in the church;
In order for the church to be united,
there must only be one teaching—
the New and Everlasting Covenant teaching,
without contamination
by the Old Covenant teaching
and human traditions.

And this gospel of the kingdom
will be preached
in the whole world as a testimony to all nations,
and then the end will come.
(Matthew 24:14 NIV)